HOLY SP

V

TABLE OF CONTENT

CHAPTER ONE

INTRODUCTION

The Holy Spirit, who is symbolized by a dove in the Sacred Scriptures and most often as a white dove in most paintings and arts, is one among the Holy Trinity and He holds great importance in Christianity. He is a protector, a guide, a light that shows Christians the right path to follow. God the Father is reasonably known and so is the Son, Jesus Christ. But when it comes to the Holy Spirit, many persons may find themselves struggling to understand who He is as well as His role in our world. In ignorance, some persons even refer to Him as an "it" or just not referred to at all. He is sometimes the forgotten or easily dismissable member of the Godhead, but this should not be the case.

According to Sacred Scriptures, the Holy Spirit played an essential and inevitable part during Christ's ministry on Earth—which could be seen right from the time when Virgin Mary conceived Him (Jesus) through the grace of the Holy Spirit according to the Gospel of Luke, to the time He breathed his last on the cross. The presence of the Holy Spirit and His power were manifest even beyond the resurrection of Jesus and up to this present time, which some persons have reckoned as the 'Era of the Holy Spirit.'

In the Old Testament era, God made a promise to pour His Spirit upon all flesh that all may receive and manifest the Spiritual gifts of the Holy Spirit. Though we are made in the image and likeness of God, the presence and gifts of the Holy Spirit in our lives is still inevitable, little wonder, even when Jesus has spent about three years with His Disciple, in spite of their three years of apprenticeship with the Master, they still were not able to do all that Jesus did. They have been well trained yet, they lacked the most important thing which was to be the completion of their apprenticeship; to experience the fulfillment of the promise God made through Prophet Joel (2:28); that in no distant time, all will receive an outpouring of the Holy Spirit and manifest the Spiritual Gifts.

The importance of Spiritual Gifts in our time cannot be overemphasized. You will remember that when Jesus and His apostles; Peter, James, and John came down from the 'Mountain of Transfiguration,' a crowd was waiting for

11

Him at the foot of the mountain because His Disciples were not able to deliver a boy suffering under a satanic yoke. I presume that the His Disciples must have tried everything they ever learned without success. After their travail, and asking why they were not able to heal (Exorcise) the boy, Jesus tells them that such calls for 'fasting and prayer' (cf. Mk 9:14-29) thereby, implying the manifestation and exercise of the gift of Word of Knowledge.

God, being an all-knowing and ever loving Father, fully aware that we need the release of Spiritual Gifts in our time, fulfilled the long-awaited promise on the Pentecost Day. Therefore, we need to note that the Spiritual Gifts are at our disposal to make human life on earth worth living. The whole Christian life is about being renewed or transformed from the inside to the outside (embracing the totality of the human person) into a divinized, glorified human being who participate correctly in precisely the same glorified human life being made manifest in Jesus Christ since he resurrected from the dead and ascended into heaven.

St. Paul teaches that "no one can say, "Jesus is Lord," except by the Holy Spirit" (1 Cor. 12:3). It is the Holy Spirit, the gift of the Risen Christ that helps us recognize the Truth. Jesus calls him the "Paraclete", meaning "the one who comes to our aid," which is by our side to support us in this journey of knowledge, and at the Last Supper, Jesus assures his disciples that the Holy Spirit will teach them all things, reminding them of his words (cf. Jn. 14:26)

This book discuses the person of the Holy Spirit; his attributes, his place in our lives, his many works, his gifts which includes the 'Sanctifying and Charismatic gifts.' The Sanctifying gifts are the gifts we receive for oneself which has the enabling graces to make such a person into another Christ. That is, qualifying him or her as it were to participate in the life of the Blessed Trinity fully. Therefore, by such we share in the grace that makes us in our small ways, sons, and daughters of God, filled with the Holy Spirit and conformed more and more to the life of Jesus.

While the CHARISMATIC GIFTS, in contrast, are the gifts the Holy Spirit give to Christians to put them on the line to help others. By implication, they are given, not to build oneself up, but so that he or she who receives any of them might build up others and renew the face of the earth. It suffices to say that such gifts reflect nature (nothing in nature is made for itself but the other) and demonstrate one of the core facts of the spiritual life: that the one chosen is chosen for the sake of the ones not chosen. For instance, the person who receives the gift of healing receives it to be a source of healing to the sick members of the body of Christ.

DEFINITION

The Holy Spirit, according to Gelasius of Cyzicus "is of the same Godhead and essence as the Father and the Son, and is ever inseparable from the Father and the Son, as the Son is from the Father, and the Father from the Son" (from the history of the Council of Nicea, A.D. 476). Epiphanius. In The Man Well-Anchore (A.D. 374), holds that the Holy Spirit is ever with the Father and the Son, and is from God, proceeding from the Father and receiving of the Son (7). Epiphanius further notes that "the Holy Spirit is neither begotten nor created but of the same substance with the Father and the Son"(Panarion, 74. A.D. 377).

According to the Athanasian Creed, the Holy Spirit is from the Father and the Son, not made nor created, nor begotten, but proceeding." (A.D. 400). Augustine says that "the Holy Spirit, according to the Holy Scriptures, is neither of the Father alone, nor of the Son alone, but of both." The Trinity, XV: 17, 27 (A.D. 408). The Holy Spirit is the third (3rd) person of the Blessed Trinity.

Knowing the Holy Spirit

The term "Spirit" translates the Hebrew word 'ruah,' which, in its primary sense, means breath, wind, and air. In John's Gospel, Jesus uses the sensory image of the wind to suggest to Nicodemus. The transcendent newness of him who is personally God's breath, the divine Spirit. On the other hand, "Spirit" and "Holy" are divine attributes common to the three divine persons. By joining the two terms, Scripture, liturgy, and theological language designate the inexpressible person of the Holy Spirit, without any possible equivocation with other uses of the terms "spirit" and "holy."

The Holy Spirit is 'the principle of every vital and truly saving action in each part of the Body.' He works in many ways to build up the Body in charity: ...by the many special graces (called 'charisms'), by which he makes the faithful 'fit and ready to undertake various tasks and offices for the renewal and building up of the Church" (CCC 798).

ORIGIN

The eternal origin of the Holy Spirit is revealed in his mission in time. The Spirit is sent to the apostles and to the Church both by the Father in the name of the son, and by the son in person, once he had returned to the Father. The fullness of the mystery of the Holy Trinity is manifest in the sending of the person of the Spirit after Jesus' glorification (CCC 244).

The Roman Catholic Church holds that Jesus announced the sending of "another Paraclete" (Advocate). The Holy Spirit, who long before the Passover, has been at work in our world, and having previously "spoken through the prophets," the Spirit will now be with and in the disciples, to teach them and guide them "into all the truth."

The Holy Spirit has been revealed as another divine person with Jesus and the Father (CCC 243). The second ecumenical council at Constantinople (381): notes that the apostolic faith concerning the Spirit was confessed. From the Creed, We believe in the Holy Spirit, the Lord and giver of life, who proceeds from the Father. By this confession, the Church holds that God the Father is the source from whom the whole divinities originate. But the origin of the Spirit is from eternity and is connected with the origin of the Son. "

The Holy Spirit, the third person of the Trinity, is God, one and equal with the Father and the Son, of the same substance and also of the same nature. However, he is not called the Spirit of the Father alone, but the Spirit of both the Father and the Son." The Creed of the Church from the Council of Constantinople confesses: "With the Father and the Son, he is worshipped and glorified (CCC 245).

CHAPTER TWO

THE PERSON OF THE HOLY SPIRIT

Who is the Holy Spirit?

In the teaching of Roman Catholic Church (CCC 264) "The Holy Spirit proceeds from the Father as the first principle and, by the eternal gift of this to the Son, from the communion of both the Father and the Son" (St. Augustine, De Trin. 15, 26, 47: PL 42, 1095). According to

Gelasius of Cyzicus, The Holy Spirit is of the same Godhead and essence as the Father and the Son, and is ever inseparable from the Father and the Son, as the Son is from the Father and the Father from the Son (History of the Council of Nicea A.D. 476). Epiphanius holds that The Holy Spirit is neither begotten nor created but of the same substance with the Father and the Son Panarion 74 (A.D. 377).

According to the Athanasian Creed (A.D. 400), The Holy Spirit is from the Father and the Son, not made nor created, nor begotten, but proceeding. Augustine, On the Trinity, XV:17,27 (A.D. 408) notes that the Holy Spirit, according to the Holy Scriptures, is neither of the Father alone, nor of the Son alone, but of both. He further paints a more precise picture when he says; wherefore let him who can understand the generation of the Son from the Father without time, also understand the procession of the Holy Spirit from both without time. More so, understand, that as the Father has in Himself that the Holy Spirit should proceed from Him, so has He given to the Son that. The same Spirit should proceed from Him, and be both apart from time: and that the Holy Spirit is so said to proceed from the Father. This should be understood that His proceeding also from the Son is a property derived by the Son from the Father. For if the Son has of the Father whatever He has, then certainly He has of the Father, that the Holy Spirit also proceeds not just from the Father alone. More so, the Spirit of both is not begotten of both but proceeds from both (A.D. 408).

Cyril of Alexandria (A.D. 430) says that the Holy Spirit is called the Spirit of Truth, and Christ is the Truth, and he is poured forth from him [the Son] just as he is also from God the Father" (Epistle 17). And the Council of Toledo II (A.D. 447) asserts that the Spirit is also the Paraclete, who is himself neither the Father and the Son, but proceeding from the Father and the Son. Therefore the Father is unbegotten, the Son is begotten, the Paraclete is not begotten, but proceeding from the Father and the Son."

The Holy Spirit is the 3rd person of the Blessed Trinity, and the one most active in the world today. The Bible says that the Holy Spirit hovered over the face of the waters at the creation of the world (Genesis 1:2), he led Jesus into the desert (Matthew 4:1), comes to us at Confirmation (Acts 8:18), and intercedes for us in sighs that we cannot understand (Romans8:26).

THE BIBLICAL SYMBOLS OF THE HOLY SPIRIT

The Scriptures uses the symbols as presented in the Catechism of the Catholic Church, to refer to the Holy Spirit; water, anointing, fire, cloud and light, the seal, the hand, the finger, the dove.

Water

The water made mention of, symbolizes the action of the Holy Spirit's in Baptism after the invocation of the Holy Spirit, the water becomes a powerful sacramental sign of new birth in Christ. In the same way, the gestation of our first birth took place in water, so too, the water of Baptism directs us to the Holy Spirit that births us into the divine life is given to us in the Holy Spirit.

As "by one Spirit we were all baptized," so we are also "made to drink of one Spirit." Thus the Spirit is also personally the living water welling up from Christ crucified as its source and welling up in us to eternal life.

Anointing

The symbolism of anointing with oil also signifies the Holy Spirit, to the point of becoming a synonym for the Holy Spirit. In Christian initiation, anointing is the sacramental sign of Confirmation, called "chrismation" in the Churches of the East. Its full force can be grasped only concerning the primary anointing accomplished by the Holy Spirit, that of Jesus. Christ (in Hebrew "messiah") means the one "anointed" by God's Spirit.

There were several anointed ones of the Lord in the Old Covenant, pre-eminently King David. But Jesus is God's Anointed in a unique way: the Holy Spirit entirely anointed the humanity the Son assumed. The Holy Spirit established him as "Christ."

The Virgin Mary conceived Christ by the Holy Spirit who, through the angel, proclaimed him the Christ at his birth, and prompted Simeon to come to the temple to see the Christ of the Lord. The Spirit-filled Christ and the power of the Spirit went out from him in his acts of healing and of saving. Finally, it was the Spirit who raised Jesus from the dead.

Now, fully established as "Christ" in his humanity victorious over death, Jesus pours out the Holy Spirit abundantly until "the saints" constitute - in their union with the humanity of the Son of God - that perfect man "to the measure of the stature of the fullness of Christ": "the whole Christ," in St. Augustine's expression.

Fire

While water signifies birth and the fruitfulness of life given in the Holy Spirit, fire symbolizes the transforming energy of the Holy Spirit's actions. The prayer of the prophet Elijah, who "arose like fire" and whose "word burned like a torch," brought down fire from heaven on the sacrifice on Mount Carmel. This event was a "figure" of the fire of the Holy Spirit, who transforms what he touches.

John the Baptist, who goes "before [the Lord] in the spirit and power of Elijah," proclaims Christ as the one who "will baptize you with the Holy Spirit and with fire." Jesus will say of the Spirit: "I came to cast fire upon the earth; and would that it was already burning!" The Roman Catholic Church holds that the symbolism of fire has been retained as one of the most expressive images of the Holy Spirit's actions. In the Acts of the Apostles, the Holy Spirit rests on the disciples on the morning of Pentecost and fills them with himself in the form of tongues "as of fire, Cloud and light." These two images occur together in the manifestations of the Holy Spirit.

In the Theophanies (manifestations of God) of the Old Testament, the cloud, now obscure, now luminous, reveals the living and saving God, while veiling the transcendence of his glory - with Moses on Mount Sinai, at the tent of meeting, and during the wandering in the desert, and with Solomon at the dedication of the Temple. In the Holy Spirit, Christ fulfills these figures. The Spirit comes upon the Virgin Mary and "overshadows" her so that she might conceive and give birth to Jesus.

On the mountain of Transfiguration, the Spirit in the "cloud came and overshadowed" Jesus, Peter, James, and

John saw Moses and Elijah and "a voice came out of the cloud, saying; 'This is my Son, my Chosen; listen to him!" Finally, the cloud took Jesus out of the sight of the disciples on the day of his ascension and will reveal him as Son of man in glory on the day of his final coming.

The seal

This symbol is close to that of anointing. "The Father has set his seal" on Christ and also seals us in him. Because this seal indicates the indelible effect of the anointing with the Holy Spirit in the sacraments of Baptism, Confirmation, and Holy Orders, the image of the seal (sphragis) has been used in some theological traditions to express the indelible "character" imprinted by these three unrepeatable sacraments.

The hand

Jesus heals the sick and blesses little children by laying hands on them. In his name, the apostles will do the same. Even more pointedly, it is by the Apostles' imposition of hands that the Holy Spirit is given. The Letter to the Hebrews lists the imposition of hands among the "fundamental elements" of its teaching. The Church has kept this sign of the all-powerful outpouring of the Holy Spirit in its sacramental epiclesis.

The finger

It is by the finger of God that Jesus cast out demons." If God's law was written on tablets of stone "by the finger of God," then the "letter from Christ" entrusted to the care of the apostles, is written, "with the Spirit of the living God, not on tablets of stone, but on tablets of human hearts." The hymn Veni Creator Spiritus invokes the Holy Spirit as the "finger of the Father's right hand."

The Dove

At the end of the flood, whose symbolism refers to Baptism, a dove released by Noah returns with a fresh olive-tree branch in its beak as a sign that the earth was again habitable. When Christ comes up from the water of his baptism, the Holy Spirit, in the form of a dove, comes down upon him and remains with him. The Spirit comes down and remains in the purified hearts of the baptized. In certain churches, the Eucharist is reserved in a metal receptacle in the form of a dove (columbarium) suspended above the altar. Christian iconography traditionally uses a dove to suggest the Spirit (CCC 694-701).

We must note that the Holy Spirit is not any of the above-listed symbols but the symbols only show an attribute or manifestation of the Holy Spirit.

THE GODHEAD

God is love: Father, Son, and Holy Spirit. God freely wills to communicate the glory of his blessed life. Such is the "plan of his loving kindness," conceived by the Father before the foundation of the world, in his beloved Son: "He destined us in love to be his sons" and "to be conformed to the image of his Son," through "the spirit of sonship. This plan is a "grace which was given to us in Christ Jesus before the ages began," stemming" immediately from Trinitarian love. It unfolds in the work of creation, the whole history of salvation after the fall, and the missions of the Son and the Spirit, which are continued in the mission of the Church (CCC 257).

There is no separation among the 'Godhead' the whole divine economy is the common work of the three divine persons. For as the Trinity has one and the same natures so too does it have only one and the same operation: "The Father, the Son, and the Holy Spirit are not three principles of creation but one principle." However, each divine person performs the common work according to his unique personal property.

Thus the Church confesses, following the New Testament, "one God and Father from whom all things are, and one Lord Jesus Christ, through whom all things are, and one Holy Spirit in whom all things are". It is above all the divine missions of the Son's Incarnation and the gift of the Holy Spirit that show forth the properties of the divine persons (CCC 258).)

Being a work at once common and personal, the whole divine economy makes known both what is proper to the divine persons, and their one divine nature. Hence the whole Christian life is a communion with each of the divine persons, without in any way separating them. Everyone who glorifies the Father does so through the Son in the Holy Spirit; everyone who follows Christ does so because the Father draws him and the Spirit moves him (CCC 259).

According to the Catechism of the Catholic Church (CCC 263-264), "The mission of the Holy Spirit, sent by the Father in the name of the Son (Jn. 14:26) and by the Son "from the Father" (Jn. 15:26), reveals that, with them, the Spirit is one and the same God. "With the Father and the Son He is worshipped and glorification (Nicene Creed). "The Holy Spirit proceeds from the Father as the first principle and, by the eternal gift of this to the Son, from the communion of both the Father and the Son" (St. Augustine, De Trin. 15, 26, 47: PL 42, 1095).

The Church further holds that "No one can say 'Jesus is Lord' except by the Holy Spirit." God has sent the Spirit of his Son into our hearts, crying, 'Abba! Father! This knowledge of faith is possible only in the Holy Spirit: to be in touch with Christ; we must first have been touched by the Holy Spirit. He comes to meet us and kindles faith in us. By virtue of our Baptism, the first sacrament of the faith, the Holy Spirit in the Church communicates to us, intimately and personally, the life that originates in the Father and is offered to us in the Son (CCC 683).

Baptism gives us the grace of new birth in God the Father, through his Son, in the Holy Spirit. For those who bear God's Spirit are led to the Word, that is, to the Son, and the Son presents them to the Father, and the Father confers incorruptibility on them. And it is impossible to see God's Son without the Spirit, and no one can approach the Father without the Son, for the knowledge of the Father is the Son, and the knowledge of God's Son is obtained through the Holy Spirit. The Old Testament proclaimed the Father clearly, but the Son more obscurely.

The New Testament revealed the Son and gave us a glimpse of the divinity of the Spirit. Now the Spirit dwells among us and grants us a clearer vision of himself. It was not prudent, when the divinity of the Father had not yet been confessed, to proclaim the Son openly and when the divinity of the Son was not yet admitted, to add the Holy Spirit as an extra burden, to speak somewhat daringly. By advancing and progressing "from glory to glory," the light of the Trinity will shine in ever more brilliant rays.

To believe in the Holy Spirit is to profess that the Holy Spirit is one of the persons of the Holy Trinity, consubstantial with the Father and the Son: "with the Father and the Son he is worshipped and glorified." For this reason, the divine mystery of the Holy Spirit was already treated in the context of Trinitarian "theology." Here, however, we have to do with the Holy Spirit only in the divine "economy" (CCC 685). Consequently, The Church, a communion living in the faith of the apostles which she transmits, is the place where we know the Holy Spirit:

- In the Scriptures he inspired; -

 In the Tradition, to which the Church Fathers are always timely witnesses;

- In the Church's Magisterium, which he assists;

- In the sacramental liturgy, through its words and symbols, in which the Holy Spirit puts us into communion with Christ;

- In prayer, wherein he intercedes for us;

- In the charisms and ministries by which the Church is built up;

- In the signs of apostolic and missionary life;

- In the witness of saints through whom he manifests his holiness and continues the work of salvation

The One whom the Father has sent into our hearts, the Spirit of his Son, is truly God. Consubstantial with the Father and the Son, the Spirit is inseparable from them, in both the inner life of the Trinity and his gift of love for the world. In adoring the Holy Trinity, life-giving, consubstantial, and indivisible, the Church's faith also professes the distinction of persons. When the Father sends his Word, he always sends his Breath. In their joint mission, the Son and the Holy Spirit are distinct but inseparable. To be sure, it is Christ who is seen, the visible image of the invisible God, but it is the Spirit who reveals him. Jesus is Christ, "anointed," because the Spirit is his anointing and everything that occurs from the Incarnation on derives from this fullness.

When Christ is finally glorified, he can, in turn, send the Spirit from his place with the Father to those who believe in him: he communicates to them his glory, that is, the Holy Spirit who glorifies him. From that time on, this joint mission will be manifested in the children adopted by the Father in the Body of his Son: the mission of the Spirit of adoption is to unite them to Christ and make them live in him:

The notion of anointing suggests that there is no distance between the Son and the Spirit. Indeed, just as between the surface of the body and the anointing with oil neither reason nor sensation recognizes any intermediary, so the contact of the Son with the Spirit is immediate so that anyone who would make contact with the Son by faith must first encounter the oil by contact. In fact, there is no part that is not covered by the Holy Spirit. That is why the confession of the Son's Lordship is made in the Holy Spirit by those who receive him, the Spirit coming from all sides to those who approach the Son in faith (CCC 688-690).

The Catechism of the Catholic Church (CCC 702) holds that from the beginning until "the fullness of time," The joint mission of the Father's Word and Spirit remains hidden, but it is at work. God's Spirit prepares for the time of the Messiah. Neither is fully revealed, but both are already promised, to be watched for and welcomed at their manifestation. So, for this reason, when the Church reads the Old Testament, she searches there for what the Spirit, "who has spoken through the prophets," wants to tell us about Christ.

By "prophets" the faith of the Church here understands all whom the Holy Spirit inspired in the composition of the sacred books, both of the Old and the New Testaments. Jewish tradition distinguishes first the Law (the five first books or Pentateuch), then the Prophets (our historical and prophetic books) and finally the Writings (especially the wisdom literature, in particular, the Psalms).

More so, according to the Church, the Holy Spirit played a distinct role in Creation, Theophanies (manifestations of God) and the Law:

Holy Spirit In creation

The Word of God and his Breath are at the origin of the being and life of every creature:

It belongs to the Holy Spirit to rule, sanctify, and animate creation, for he is God, consubstantial with the Father and the Son. Power over life pertains to the Spirit, for being God he preserves creation in the Father through the Son (CCC 703).

The Spirit of the promise

Disfigured by sin and death, humanity remains "in the image of God," in the image of the Son, but is deprived "of the glory of God," of his "likeness." The promise made to Abraham inaugurates the economy of salvation, at the culmination of which the Son himself will assume that "image" and restore it in the Father's "likeness" by giving it again its Glory, the Spirit who is "the giver of life." Against all human hope, God promises descendants to Abraham, as the fruit of faith and the power of the Holy Spirit. In Abraham's progeny, all the nations of the earth will be blessed. This progeny will be Christ himself, in whom the outpouring of the Holy Spirit will "gather into one the children of God who are scattered abroad." God commits himself by his solemn oath to giving his beloved Son and "the promised Holy Spirit who is the guarantee of our inheritance until we acquire possession of it." (CCC 705-706)

In Theophanies and the Law
Theophanies (manifestations of God) light up the way of the promise, from the patriarchs to Moses and from Joshua to the visions that inaugurated the missions of the great prophets. Christian tradition has always recognized that God's Word allowed himself to be seen and heard in these theophanies, in which the cloud of the Holy Spirit both revealed him and concealed him in its shadow (CCC 707).

The Church holds that "There was a man sent from God, whose name was John." John was filled with the Holy

Spirit even from his mother's womb by Christ himself, whom the Virgin Mary had just conceived by the Holy Spirit. Mary's visitation to Elizabeth thus became a visit from God to his people. John is "Elijah (who) must come." The fire of the Spirit dwells in him and makes him the forerunner of the coming Lord. In John, the precursor, the Holy Spirit completes the work of "[making] ready a people prepared for the Lord. John the Baptist is "more than a prophet." In him, the Holy Spirit concludes his speaking through the prophets. John completes the cycle of prophets begun by Elijah.

He proclaims the imminence of the consolation of Israel; he is the "voice" of the Consoler who is coming. As the Spirit of truth will also do, John "came to bear witness to the light." In John's sight, the Spirit thus brings to completion the careful search of the prophets and fulfills the longing of the angels. "He on whom you see the Spirit descend and remain, this is he who baptizes with the Holy Spirit. And I have seen and have borne witness that this is the Son of God.... Behold, the Lamb of God." Finally, with John the Baptist, the Holy Spirit begins the restoration to man of "the divine likeness," prefiguring what he would achieve with and in Christ. John's baptism was for repentance; baptism in water and the Spirit will be a new birth (CCC 717-720).

The Spouse of the Holy Spirit

The Church equally teaches that Mary, the all-holy ever-virgin Mother of God, is the masterwork of the mission of the Son and the Spirit in the fullness of time. For the first time in the plan of salvation and because his Spirit had prepared her, the Father found the dwelling place where his Son and his Spirit could dwell among men. In this sense, the Church's Tradition has often read the most beautiful texts on wisdom about Mary.

Mary is acclaimed and represented in the liturgy as the "Seat of Wisdom." In her, the "wonders of God" that the Spirit was to fulfill in Christ and the Church began to be made manifest. The Holy Spirit prepared Mary by his grace. It fitted that the mother of him in whom "the whole fullness of deity dwells bodily" should herself be "full of grace." She was, by sheer grace, conceived without sin as the most humble of creatures, the most capable of welcoming the inexpressible gift of the Almighty. It was quite correct for the angel Gabriel to greet her as the "Daughter of Zion": "Rejoice." It is the thanksgiving of the whole People of God, and thus of the Church, which Mary in her canticle lifts up to the Father in the Holy Spirit while carrying within her the eternal Son. In Mary, the Holy Spirit fulfills the plan of the Father's loving goodness.

With and through the Holy Spirit, the Virgin conceives and gives birth to the Son of God. By the Holy Spirit's power and her faith, her virginity became uniquely fruitful. In Mary, the Holy Spirit manifests the Son of the Father, now become the Son of the Virgin.

She is the burning bush of the definitive theophany. Filled with the Holy Spirit, she makes the Word visible in the humility of his flesh. It is to the poor and the first representatives of the gentiles that she makes him known. Finally, through Mary, the Holy Spirit begins to bring men, the objects of God's merciful love, into communion with Christ, and the humble are always the first to accept him:

shepherds, magi, Simeon and Anna, the bride and groom at Cana, and the first disciples (CCC 721-725).

However, the Church in her teaching holds that Jesus does not reveal the Holy Spirit fully until He has been glorified through his Death and Resurrection. Nevertheless, little by little he alludes to him even in his teaching of the multitudes, as when he reveals that his flesh will be food for the life of the world. He also alludes to the Spirit in speaking to Nicodemus, to the Samaritan woman, and to those who take part in the feast of Tabernacles.

To his disciples he speaks openly of the Spirit in connection with prayer and with the witness, they will have to bear. Only when the hour has arrived for his glorification does Jesus promise the coming of the Holy Spirit, since his Death and Resurrection will fulfill the promise made to the fathers. The Spirit of truth, the other Paraclete, will be given by the Father in answer to Jesus' prayer; he will be sent by the Father in Jesus' name, and Jesus will send him from the Father's side since he comes from the Father. The Holy Spirit will come, and we shall know him; he will be with us forever; he will remain with us.

The Spirit will teach us everything, remind us of all that Christ said to us and bear witness to him. The Holy Spirit will lead us into all truth and will glorify Christ. He will prove the world wrong about sin, righteousness, and judgment. At last Jesus' hour arrives: he commends his spirit into the Father's hands at the very moment when by his death he conquers death, so that "raised from the dead by the glory of the Father," he might immediately give the Holy Spirit by "breathing" on his disciples.

From this hour onward, the mission of Christ and the Spirit becomes the mission of the Church: "As the Father has sent me, even so, I send you." (CCC 728-730).

Moreover, "God is Love," and love is his first gift, containing all others. "God's love has been poured into our hearts through the Holy Spirit whom God gives to us." cause we are dead or at least wounded through sin, the first effect of the gift of love is the forgiveness of our sins.

The communion of the Holy Spirit in the Church restores to the baptized the divine likeness lost through sin. He, then, gives us the "pledge" or "first fruits" of our inheritance: the very life of the Holy Trinity, which is to love as "God has loved us." This love (the "charity" of 1 Cor. 13) is the source of the new life in Christ, made possible because we have received "power" from the Holy Spirit. By this power of the Spirit, God's children can bear much fruit. He who has grafted us onto the true vine will make us bear "the fruit of the Spirit: love, joy, peace, patience, kindness, goodness, faithfulness, gentleness, self-control." We live by the Spirit; the more we renounce ourselves, the more we "walk by the Spirit."

Through the Holy Spirit, we are restored to paradise, led back to the Kingdom of heaven, and adopted as children, given the confidence to call God "Father" and to share in Christ's grace, called children of light and given a share in eternal glory

The mission of Christ and the Holy Spirit is brought to completion in the Church, which is the Body of Christ and the Temple of the Holy Spirit. This joint mission henceforth brings Christ's faithful to share in his communion with the Father in the Holy Spirit.

The Spirit prepares men and goes out to them with his grace, in order to draw them to Christ. The Spirit manifests the risen Lord to them, recalls his word to them and opens their minds to the understanding of his Death and Resurrection. He makes present the mystery of Christ, supremely in the Eucharist, in order to reconcile them, to bring them into communion with God, that they may "bear much fruit."

Thus the Church's mission is not an addition to that of Christ and the Holy Spirit, but is its sacrament: in her whole being and in all her members, the Church is sent to announce, bear witness, make present, and spread the mystery of the communion of the Holy Trinity: According to St. Cyril of Alexandria, "All of us who have received one and the same Spirit, that is, the Holy Spirit, are in a sense blended together with one another and with God. For if Christ, together with the Father's and his own Spirit, comes to dwell in each of us, though we are many, still the Spirit is one and undivided. He binds together the spirits of each and every one of us, and makes all appear as one in him. For just as the power of Christ's sacred flesh unites those in whom it dwells into one body, I think that in the same way the one and undivided Spirit of God, who dwells in all, leads all into spiritual unity".

Because the Holy Spirit is the anointing of Christ, it is Christ who, as the head of the Body, pours out the Spirit among his members to nourish, heal, and organize them in their mutual functions, to give them life, send them to bear witness, and associate them to his self-offering to the Father and to his intercession for the whole world. Through the Church's sacraments, Christ communicates his Holy and sanctifying Spirit to the members of his Body. (CCC 733-739).

The Spirit helps us in our weakness; for we do not know how to pray as we ought, but the Spirit himself intercedes with sighs too deep for words. The Holy Spirit, the artisan of God's works, is the master of prayer (CCC 741).The Holy Spirit, whom Christ the head pours out on his members, builds, animates, and sanctifies the Church. She is the sacrament of the Holy Trinity's communion with men (CCC747).

CHAPTER THREE

THE ROLE OF THE HOLY SPIRIT

The role of the Holy Spirit in the lives of Christians is quite outstanding. Little wonder, Jesus insists that it is expedient that he goes away to usher in the reign of the 'Paraclete.' This was evident the night before Jesus' crucifixion. Confused and filled with grief, the disciples struggled to comprehend their Savior's words. Was he going away? How? Why? They had walked closely with the Son of Man, seen Him perform countless miracles, heard him teach like no other Rabbi and yet, now He spoke of leaving. Can you imagine their distress? Fear? Disillusionment?

Christ chose this pivotal moment to prepare His beloved disciples for the coming Holy Spirit. "But very truly I tell you, it is for your good that I am going away. Unless I go away, the Advocate will not come to you; but if I go, I will send him to you." John 16:7 (NIV). Jesus told His disciples what seemed inconceivable at the time; His absence was a good thing. But how could this be? Who would not want the Savior close? The luxury of being able to walk and talk with Jesus physically seemed to fail in comparison to the promised "Advocate."

Pope Francis teaches that the action of the Holy Spirit in our lives, and the life of the Church to guide us to the truth is, first of all, to remind and imprint on the hearts of believers the words that Jesus said, and precisely through these words, God's law – as the prophets of the Old Testament had announced – is inscribed in our hearts and becomes within us a principle of evaluation in our choices and of guidance in our daily actions, it becomes a principle of life. Ezekiel's great prophecy is realized: "I will sprinkle clean water over you to make you clean; from all your impurities and from all your idols I will cleanse you. I will give you a new heart, and a new spirit I will put within you. ...I will put my spirit within you so that you walk in my statutes, observe my ordinances, and keep them" (36:25-27). Indeed, our actions are born from deep within: it is the heart that needs to be converted to God, and the Holy Spirit transforms it if we open ourselves to Him.

His Place in the Life of Christians

The disciples could not understand that Christ was limited by His human nature. He could not be everywhere at once. It took time to travel from location to location. For instance, when Jairus' only daughter was dying, Jesus had to walk to get to her. On the way, He was slowed down by the crowd. And as if that was not enough, before He got there He was stopped by a woman with an urgent issue of blood. So, it is evident that He had physical limitations.

Although Jesus was restricted by His humanity here on earth, the promised Holy Spirit would not be. He would bypass man's physical constraints by dwelling inside the hearts of humanity. Just as it says in, 1 Corinthians 3:16 (NIV), "Do you not know that you are a temple of God and that the Spirit of God dwells in you?" Jesus attempted to convey the physical change that was about to take place. The sovereign God of the universe would make his home inside ordinary and sin-prone human beings. Unfortunately, the disciples did not understand that the "Advocate" Christ mentioned was God Himself.

Whatever your need may be, Inviting the Holy Spirit into your life, your body, and your house will change your life in ways you cannot imagine. This is sure to happen, especially if you are tired of the world beating down on you all the time. Without warning, you will start gaining insights and solutions to problems that you have. All of a sudden, things that you never saw before your very eyes would become plain as day. Answers to your most significant problems pop into your head when you least expect them. As Jesus assures us that; "When he, the Spirit of truth comes, he will guide you into all the truth.

He will not give His message but will speak only of what He hears, and He will declare to you the things to come" (John 16:13).

The Holy Spirit makes all the difference; He makes seemingly impossible things possible. Maybe you cannot pay off your bills, invoke the Holy Spirit. Can you not get along with your spouse? Invoke the Holy Spirit. You may have been out of a job or cannot get a good one, invoke the Holy Spirit. You may have been stuck up and cannot stop looking at pornography, invoke the Holy Spirit. Or you need healing of; body, mind, soul, emotions or relationship, invoke the Holy Spirit.

It is a truth that inviting the Holy Spirit to take over your life is the strength for the journey of the rest of your life! Little wonder, Jesus being fully aware of the place of the Holy Spirit admonished his disciple before his Ascension into heaven saying, "Do not leave Jerusalem but wait for the fulfillment of the Father's promise about which I have spoken to you; for John baptized with water, but you will be baptized with the Holy Spirit within a few days" (Acts 1:4-5). Let's not forget that the disciples in question had been with Jesus from the beginning of his public ministry, which would imply that they must have been well taught by Jesus, their Master, yet he tells them to 'wait.' This presupposes that they needed much more than being taught the ways and business of the Master.

They had to walk the face of the earth not just as those who have been trained by Jesus and have known the business of the Master, but as another Jesus Christ. As such, we need to be endued with power from 'On-High'. To this effect, Jesus says "But you will receive power when the Holy Spirit comes upon you; and you will be my witnesses in Jerusalem, throughout Judea and Samaria and to the ends of the earth" (Acts 1:8). As a proof of the difference the Holy Spirit makes in our lives, you may look at how Peter's life was changed when the Holy Spirit took over his life; he went from being a weak Jesus-denying coward to become a fearless Evangelizer.

The same thing can happen to every one of us! All of these changes may not happen immediately but in God's good time. After all, no crop or plant bears fruit the same day it is planted, but it undergoes specific processes. But who helps us recognize that Jesus is "the" Word of truth, the only begotten Son of God the Father?

St. Paul teaches that "no one can say, "Jesus is Lord," except by the Holy Spirit" (1 Cor. 12:3). It is the Holy Spirit, the gift of the Risen Christ that helps us recognize the Truth. Jesus calls him the "Paraclete", meaning "the one who comes to our aid," and is by our side to support us in this journey of knowledge, and at the Last Supper, Jesus assures his disciples that the Holy Spirit will teach them all things, reminding them of his words (cf. Jn. 14:26).

What is then the action of the Holy Spirit in our lives and in the life of the Church to guide us to the truth? First of all, remind and imprint on the hearts of believers the words that Jesus said, and precisely through these words, God's law as the prophets of the Old Testament had announced is inscribed in our hearts and becomes within us a principle of evaluation in our choices and of guidance in our daily actions, it becomes a principle of life. Ezekiel's great prophecy is realized: "I will sprinkle clean water over you to make you clean; from all your impurities and all your idols I will cleanse you. I will give you a new heart, and a new spirit I will put within you. ...I will put my spirit within you so that you walk in my statutes, observe my ordinances, and keep them" (36:25-27). Indeed, our actions are born from deep within: it is the heart that needs to be converted to God, and the Holy Spirit transforms it if we open ourselves to Him.

The Holy Spirit, as Jesus promises, guides us "into all truth" (Jn. 16:13) he leads us not only to an encounter with Jesus, the fullness of Truth but guides us "into" the Truth, that is, he helps us enter into a deeper communion with Jesus himself, gifting us knowledge of the things of God. We cannot achieve this on our strengths. If God does not enlighten us interiorly, our being Christians will be superficial.

The Tradition of the Church affirms that the Spirit of truth acts in our hearts, provoking that "sense of faith" (Sensus Fidei), through which, as the Second Vatican Council affirms, the People of God, under the guidance of the Magisterium, adheres unwaveringly to the faith given once and for all to the people of God, penetrates it more deeply with right thinking, and applies it more fully in its life (cf. Lumen Gentium 12).

Today, how many of us are open to the Holy Spirit? How many pray to Him to enlighten them, to make them more sensitive to the things of God? According to Pope Francis, "this is a prayer we need to pray every day, every day: Holy Spirit may my heart be open to the Word of God, may my heart be open to good, may my heart be open to the beauty of God, every day." But so many Christians are more preoccupied with 'give me this or that' kind of prayer rather than turn to the Holy Spirit for insight on how to truly enjoy life. To make this point more explicit, the Gospel of Luke brings to mind the action of the Virgin Mary who "kept all these things and pondered them in her heart" (Lk.2: 19, 51).

Pope Francis notes that the reception of the words and the truths of faith so that they become life is realized and grows under the action of the Holy Spirit. In this sense, we must learn from Mary, reliving her "yes", her total availability to receive the Son of God in her life, and who from that moment was transformed. Through the Holy Spirit, the Father and the Son come to dwell in us: do we live in God and of God? Is our life animated by God?

Through his grace, the Holy Spirit is the first to awaken faith in us and to communicate to us the new life, which is to "know the Father and the one whom he has sent, Jesus Christ." But the Spirit is the last of the persons of the Holy Trinity to be revealed. St. Gregory of Nazianzus, the Theologian, explains this progression regarding the pedagogy of divine "condescension" (CCC 684).

The Holy Spirit is at work with the Father and the Son from the beginning to the completion of the plan for our salvation. But in these "end times," ushered in by the Son's redeeming Incarnation, the Spirit is revealed and given, recognized and welcomed as a person. Now can this divine plan, accomplished in Christ, the firstborn and head of the new creation, be embodied in humanity by the outpouring of the Spirit: as the Church, the communion of saints, the forgiveness of sins, the resurrection of the body, and the life everlasting" (CCC 686).

The Catechism of the Catholic Church adds that "Now God's Spirit, who reveals God, makes known to us Christ, his Word, his living Utterance, but the Spirit does not speak of himself. The Spirit who "has spoken through the prophets" makes us hear the Father's Word, but we do not hear the Spirit himself. We know him only in the movement by which he reveals the Word to us and disposes us to welcome him in faith. The Spirit of truth who "unveils" Christ to us "will not speak on his own." Such properly divine self-effacement explains why "the world cannot receive (him), because it neither sees him nor knows him," while those who believe in Christ know the Spirit because he dwells with them (CCC 687).

It is a truth that "No one can say 'Jesus is Lord' except by the Holy Spirit." Every time we begin to pray to Jesus, it is the Holy Spirit who draws us on the way of prayer by his prevenient grace. Since he teaches us to pray by recalling Christ, how could we not pray to the Spirit too? That is why the Church invites us to call upon the Holy Spirit every day, especially at the beginning and the end of every significant action (CCC 2670). The Holy Spirit, whose anointing permeates our whole being, is the interior Master of Christian prayer. He is the artisan of the living tradition of prayer. To be sure, there are as many paths of prayer as there are persons who pray, but it is the same Spirit acting in all and with all. It is in the communion of the Holy Spirit that Christian prayer is prayer in the Church. In prayer, the Holy Spirit unites us to the person of the only, in his glorified humanity, through which and in which our filial prayer unites us in the Church with the Mother of Jesus (CCC 2672-2673).

Consequently, in Sacred Scripture, God humanly speaks to man. To interpret Sacred Scripture correctly, the reader must be attentive to what the human authors truly wanted to affirm, and to what God wanted to reveal to us by their words. To discover the sacred authors' intention, the reader must take into account the conditions of their time and culture, the literary genres in use at that time, and the modes of feeling, speaking and narrating then current. "For the fact is that truth is differently presented and expressed in the various types of historical writing, in prophetical and poetical texts, and in other forms of literary expression." But since Sacred Scripture is inspired, there is another and no less important principle of correct interpretation, without which Scripture would remain a dead letter. "Sacred Scripture must be read and interpreted in the light of the same Spirit by whom it was written" (CCC 109-111)

Do not be a 'part-time" Christian, at certain moments, in certain circumstances, and in certain choices, be a Christian at all times! The truth of Christ that the Holy Spirit teaches us and gives us always and forever involves our daily lives. Let us invoke him more often, to guide us on the path of Christ's disciples.

The Function of the Holy Spirit in the Life of Believers
He Convicts and Regenerates Our Spirit

The Holy Spirit is very active when it comes to convicting us of our sin; He shows us that none of us can live up to the righteousness of Jesus, and reveals to us the judgment that is coming to those who die without a Savior (cf. John 16:8-11). When we repent, confess our sins and receive the gift of Salvation, the Holy Spirit regenerates our dead inner human spirit, which now becomes sensitive to the spiritual things of God (cf. John 3:1-16; and Acts 2:38). This is referred to in the Bible as the "New Birth."

Believers Receive Him Wholly

At baptism when we received the Holy Spirit, we receive all the Holy Spirit we will ever receive. He does not come in pieces and parts. He is either in us or not (cf. Acts 1:4-5; and 1 Corinthians 12:13). At the same moment, the Holy Spirit baptizes or immerses us into the family of God the worldwide followers of Christ past, present, and future.

He is Our Comforter

As one of the attributes of the Holy Spirit, He brings peace in the midst of storms. He is our encourager and comforter when we are hurting and discouraged.

Sometimes the only place we can go is to the Spirit of Jesus the Holy Spirit who gives us peace and comforts us (cf. John 14:16-17, 16:7 Ephesians 2:14; Philippians 4:7).

He Empowers Believers to Live Righteously

As the Scripture says; "by strength shall no man prevail." The Holy Spirit pours into us the power for victorious living. If you are in the hospital for surgery, instead of fear and fretting, you find peace and contentment through the Holy Spirit who pours into you the grace and power that you need (Romans 8:26; Philippians 4:10-13). He also empowers and inspires us for evangelization.

He Enables Believers to Read the Bible and Pray

As the Spiritual author of the Bible who inspires the human authors (cf. 2 Tim 3:16), He teams with us in studying, and He gives us the understanding of the truths of the Bible. After all, who teaches better and interprets the Bible for us than the one who wrote the Book? (John 14:25, 16:12-15) Every passage in Scripture has only one, right interpretation. It is the Spirit that guides us to figure out what the Bible writer had in mind when he wrote what he wrote.

More so, not only does the Holy Spirit guide our prayers, He steps in to intercede for us when we cannot put our feelings into words (cf. Romans 8:26). Even sometimes, when our pain is so deep that we can only groan, He turns our groans into prayers.

The Holy Spirit is Our Ever Present Help

In the Greek, Advocate means Parakleton, or someone called alongside to help and strengthen. Even though no English word can succinctly capture the full meaning of the word, other translations use Helper, Counselor, and Comforter. The Holy Spirit exists in the life of the believer to be an ever-present help.

He is also known as the "Spirit of Truth." In John 16:13(NIV) Jesus further describes the Holy Spirit by saying, "But when he, the Spirit of truth, comes, he will guide you into all the truth. He will not speak on his own; he will speak only what he hears, and he will tell you what is yet to come. "In addition to comforting believers, He is a truth compass: guiding believers as we navigate the lies this world bombards us with daily. He is able to sort through deception lurking in our own hearts: convicting us of sin, revealing the truth and illuminating righteousness.

The Holy Spirit is the Source of Power for Evangelization
He is also a power source. Acts1:8 (NIV) quotes the words of Jesus before He ascended to heaven, "But you will receive power when the Holy Spirit comes on you, and you will be my witnesses in Jerusalem, and in all Judea and Samaria, and to the ends of the earth."

Just as Christ foretold, the disciples received power on the day of Pentecost when the Holy Spirit came in like a "violent wind" and filled them with His presence. Instantaneously He enabled them to speak in different tongues. This occurrence was necessary for the spreading of the Gospel of Jesus Christ.

The Holy Spirit still works in the lives of believers today. He is a helper and counselor, "the Spirit of Truth" and a power source. If we are going to live impactful lives on this earth must know Him and the benefits He brings to the life of every believer.

CHAPTER FOUR

BIBLICAL ACCOUNTS OF THE HOLY SPIRIT

The Holy Spirit has been mentioned severally in the Bible, both in the Old Testament and the New Testament. Isaiah in his book (cf.11:1-5) presents to us the Sanctifying gifts of the Holy Spirit. These gifts are essential for every Christian, as without them, it will be impossible for us to be the true image of Christ.

As Christ's image, you have the divine enablement which disposes you to build yourself up and to help the others just as Jesus helps us. It takes your becoming as wise, understanding, compassionate, courageous, and righteous as Jesus was when He walked the face of the earth. It is only because of these virtues that He could look past the complexities of this mundane world that distract our human hearts and minds through temptation, greed, and futile ambitions that are limited to the material world. It is these seven gifts that can help us understand the true meaning of being His disciples and to get to know Him more closely, in His right image.

Holy Spirit in the Old Testament

There is no doubt that no clearer statement of the intimate interworking of the triune God; Father, Son and Holy Spirit and especially of the Spirit's powerful role can be found in the Old Testament than in Isaiah's prophecy of the Servant of the Lord (Is. 42:1–9). The text summarizes the redeeming work of all three Persons of the Trinity in the salvation of humanity. However, the book of Isaiah ties together in remarkable harmony both the Old

Testament and New Testament understandings of God's grace. It also sheds light on our understanding of the Holy Spirit. Some Bible readers assume that the Holy Spirit's activity in Scripture is limited to the New Testament. But not quite actually, He is just as active in the Old Testament as we can affirm from the following Scriptural texts:

WORKS OF THE HOLY SPIRIT IN THE OLD TESTAMENT

For a clearer understanding, let us consider some notable and remarkable works of the Holy Spirit in the Old Testament though not in any specific order:

In the Book of Genesis

1. The book of Genesis gives a clear proof that the Spirit of God participated in creation (cf. Gen. 1:2; Job 26:13; Is. 32:15) Genesis 1:1-2 - "In the beginning, God created the heavens and the earth. Now the earth was formless and empty, darkness was over the surface of the deep, and the Spirit of God was hovering over the waters.

In Genesis 6:3, He is presented as the Spirit that strives with sinners, which is perhaps related to His work in convicting people of sin; "Then the LORD said, "My Spirit will not contend with man forever, for he is mortal; his days will be a hundred and twenty years." And going further in Genesis 41:38, we find an allusion made to Him as the great 'revealer of mysteries' after Joseph interprets Pharaoh's dream which none else could interpret. "So Pharaoh asked them, Can we find anyone like this man, one in whom is the spirit of God?" The Spirit gives life to humanity and the other creatures (Ps. 104:29, 30). It is interesting that when Genesis says God endows people with life by breathing into their nostrils the "breath of life" (Gen. 2:7), the word for "breath" is the same word translated elsewhere as "spirit."

The author of the book of Psalm (Psalm 104:30) notes that; "When you send your Spirit, they are created, and you renew the face of the earth."

During the time of the patriarchs
1.   The Spirit came upon certain judges, warriors, and prophets at certain times in history in a way that they received extraordinary powers. Among such persons

include; Joshua as recorded in the book of Numbers (27:18), Othniel as recorded in the book of Judges (6:10), Gideon (6:34), and Samson (13:25; 14:6). The first book of Samuel (10:9, 10) presents us with Saul who receives the Spirit too. However, the Spirit later departed from Saul because of his disobedience (16:14).

2. We also see the prominent role played by the Spirit in the long span of Old Testament prophecy. According to the second book of Samuel (23:2), David declares that "the Spirit of the Lord spoke by me, and His word was on my tongue. In the same vein, in the book of Ezekiel (2:2), he (Ezekiel) reports that "the Spirit entered me when He spoke to me."

3. The work of inspiring holiness in Old Testament believers is also attributed to the Spirit (cf. Ps. 143:10). And because the role of the Spirit in the lives of human beings is inevitable and irreplaceable, Ezekiel notes that someday God would put His Spirit in His people in a way that would cause them to live according to His statutes (cf. Ezek. 36:27).

4.   In the book of Isaiah, the author presents the Spirit as being crucial in helping God's people anticipate the ministry of the Messiah. For example, Isaiah 11:1–5 is a Trinitarian preview of the working of the Father, the Spirit, and the Son, who is the Branch of Jesse. Looking forward to the ministry of Jesus Christ, the Holy Spirit inspired Isaiah to prophesy: "The Spirit of the Lord shall rest upon Him" (Is. 11:2), inspiring God's Chosen One with wisdom, understanding, counsel, fortitude, knowledge, fear of the Lord, righteousness, and faithfulness. However, we come full cycle to the New Testament, where Jesus appropriates the Old Testament prophecies claiming to be the fulfillment of the prophecy (cf. Is. 61:1, 2; Luke 4:18, 19).

He gives the Grace of Leadership
In the book of Numbers chapter 11:16-30, we read of how God has previously given His Spirit to Moses had to extend the grace of leadership to others; "The LORD said to Moses: 'Bring me seventy of Israel's elders who are known to you as leaders and officials among the people. Have them come to the Tent of Meeting that they may stand there with you.

I will come down and speak with you there, and I will take of the Spirit that is on you and put the Spirit on them. They will help you carry the burden of the people so that you will not have to carry it alone. So Moses went out and told the people what the LORD had said. He brought together seventy of their elders and had them stand around the Tent. Then the LORD came down in the cloud and spoke with him, and he took of the Spirit that was on him and put the Spirit on the seventy elders. When the Spirit rested on them, they prophesied, but they did not do so again. However, two men, whose names were Eldadand Medad, had remained in the camp. They were listed among the elders but did not go out to the Tent.

However, the Spirit also rested on them, and they prophesied in the camp. A young man ran and told Moses, 'Eldad and Medad are prophesying in the camp. Joshua, son of Nun, who had been Moses aide since youth, spoke up and said, 'Moses, my lord, stop them!' But Moses replied, 'Are you jealous for my sake? I wish that all the LORD's people were prophets and that the LORD would put his Spirit on them!' Then Moses and the elders of Israel returned to the camp."

The author of the book of Numbers also notes that Joshua received the Spirit (Numbers 27:18); "So the LORD said to Moses, "Take Joshua son of Nun, a man in whom is the spirit, and lay your hand on him."

The Spirit Gives Different Abilities

The author of the book of Exodus (31:1-5) notes that; He granted the artistic and technical skills to construct the temple. "Then the LORD said to Moses, "See, I have chosen Bezalel son of Uri, the son of Hur, of the tribe of Judah, and I have filled him with the Spirit of God, with skill, ability, and knowledge in all kinds of crafts - to make artistic designs for work in gold, silver and bronze, to cut and set stones, to work in wood, and to engage in all kinds of craftsmanship." 12. He gave Ability and Grace to lead.

The book of Judges 3:10 say about 'Othniel' that "The Spirit of the LORD came upon him so that he became Israel's judge and went to war. The LORD gave Cushan-Rishathaim king of Aram into the hands of Othniel, who overpowered him" (Judges 6:34). "Then the Spirit of the LORD came upon Gideon, and he blew a trumpet, summoning the Abiezrites to follow him" (Judges 11:29). Still, in the book of Judges, we find the account of Jephthah "Then the Spirit of the LORD came upon Jephthah. He crossed Gilead and Manasseh, passed through Mizpah of Gilead, and from there he advanced against the Ammonites" (Judges 13:25).

Concerning Samson, the book of Judges says that "The Spirit of the LORD began to stir him while he was in Mahaneh Dan, between Zorah and Eshtaol"(Judges 14:6). "The Spirit of the LORD came upon him in power so that he tore the lion apart with his bare hands as he might have torn a young goat. But he told neither his father nor his mother what he had done" (Judges 14:19-20).

"Then the Spirit of the LORD came upon him in power. He went down to Ashkelon, struck down thirty of their men, stripped them of their belongings and gave their clothes to those who had explained the riddle. Burning with anger, he went up to his father's house" (Judges 15:14). "As he approached Lehi, the Philistines came toward him shouting, then the Spirit of the LORD came upon him in power. The ropes on his arms became like charred flax, and the bindings dropped from his hands."

Leadership Ability

The Spirit assisted the first kings of Israel in their task of guiding the people of God. (1 Samuel 10:6); "The Spirit of the LORD will come upon you in power, and you will prophesy with them, and you will be changed into a different person."

"So Samuel took the horn of oil and anointed him in the presence of his brothers, and from that day on the Spirit of the LORD came upon David in power (1Samuel 16:13-14). Samuel then went to Ramah. Now the Spirit of the LORD had departed from Saul, and an evil spirit from the LORD tormented him." In the second book of Samuel (23:2) - "The Spirit of the LORD spoke through me; his word was on my tongue."

The book of Numbers says (Numbers 11:25); "Then the LORD came down in the cloud and spoke with him, and he took of the Spirit that was on him and put the Spirit on the seventy elders. When the Spirit rested on them, they prophesied, but they did not do so again." Going further, (Numbers 24:2); "When Balaam looked out and saw Israel encamped tribe by tribe, the Spirit of God came upon him" and he prophesied.

The book of Nehemiah (Nehemiah 9:30) says; "For many years you were patient with them. By your Spirit, you admonished them through your prophets. Yet they paid no attention, so you handed them over to the neighboring peoples."

Acknowledging the power of the Spirit, Isaiah (Isaiah 48:16) says; "Come near me and listen to this 'From the first announcement I have not spoken in secret; at the time it happens, I am there.' And now the Sovereign LORD has sent me, with his Spirit."

Still considering the power of the Spirit, Micah (Micah 3:8) notes; "But as for me, I am filled with power, with the Spirit of the LORD, and with justice and might, to declare to Jacob his transgression, to Israel his sin."

Ezekiel is not left out in experiencing the power of the Spirit, he says (Ezekiel 2:2); "As he spoke, the Spirit came into me and raised me to my feet, and I heard him speaking to me."

It is important to understand that the Holy Spirit did not work directly with all the people in the Old Testament even though there was a promise that He would come to all one day. Nor did He always cause the person to be Holy. The "human vessels" used by God in the Old Testament were often very sinful and unclean as in the cases of Balaam and Samson. The Spirit was mainly given to the prophets and others who would be vehicles of divine revelation.

He also granted gifts to manage, to practice arts and skills, to lead, to judge and even to use physical force. In the Old Testament, there are many references to the person and work of the Spirit. Some of the texts indicate that, at that time, the Spirit came to do a specific task and left when His work was done. While In the New Testament, we will see that His presence became permanent and constant.

The Holy Spirit In the New Testament

The New Testament shows that the Holy Spirit is vitally involved in the development of the church. The revelation of the Holy Spirit as a distinct person from the Father and the Son, who is not explicitly presented in the Old Testament, becomes very explicit in the New Testament.

It is true that the New Testament writings do not offer us a step by step teaching on the Holy Spirit. However, it gives us all that we need to understand and relate with Him (Holy Spirit). Jesus announces the gift of the Spirit as he completes his earthly work: 'When the Paraclete comes, the Spirit of truth who comes from the Father – and whom I will send from the Father – he will bear witness on my behalf. You must bear witness as well, for you have been with me from the beginning" (Jn. 15:26ff.).

But before this time, He insists that the Holy Spirit is inevitable in our lives when He says that "it is better for you that I go away..." (Jn. 16:7). This same Spirit will sustain the evangelizing mission of the Church, as Jesus had promised his disciples: "Behold, I send the promise of my Father upon you; but stay in the city, until you are clothed with power from on high" (Lk. 24:49).

The Holy Spirit in the Gospels Mathew's Gospel

In the four Gospels, we see that the Holy Spirit is given a prominent place beginning with the Gospel of Mathew which in chapter one notes that it was through the power of the Holy Spirit that Mary conceived (cf.18, 20), Mathew also holds that the Holy Spirit participated in the baptism of Jesus (cf. Mt 3:16) after which He (Holy Spirit) led Jesus into the wilderness to be tempted by the devil (cf. Mt 4:1ff), implying that the Holy Spirit empowered Jesus to be victorious.

Still talking about the function of the Holy Spirit, Mathew says that John the Baptist announced that Jesus would baptize his followers with the Holy Spirit and fire (cf. Mt

73

3:11). Mathew attributed the success of Jesus' public ministry to the Holy Spirit and that he cast out demons by the power of the Holy Spirit (cf. Mt 12:28).

Marks Gospel

The Gospel of Mark being one of the Synoptic Gospels also presents the Holy Spirit as the power behind the success of Jesus in His ministry. Mark omits the miraculous conception and birth of Jesus Christ but presents the account of His baptism where he depicts the Holy Spirit as a dove (one of the symbols of the Holy) that descended on Jesus (cf.1:9-10) as He came out of the river Jordan. Mark equally talks about the leading role of the Holy Spirit (cf.1:12).

Luke's Gospel

The Gospel of look gives a broader account of the activity of the Holy Spirit in the life and ministry of Jesus Christ. If we compare the Synoptic Gospels with regards to teachings and actions of the Holy Spirit, the Evangelist Luke offers a far more advanced study. The account begins with Jesus' forerunner, John the Baptist, who according to the text was himself filled with the Holy Spirit from his mother's womb (cf. 1:15).

The Gospel of Luke gives a more detailed account of the role of the Holy Spirit in the conception of Virgin Mary (cf. 1:26-38).In this Gospel, the function of the Holy Spirit as the one who 'reveals mysteries' is presented in the account of Mary's visit to her cousin, Elizabeth (cf. 1:41-45). And in the account of the Presentation of Jesus in the Temple (cf. 2:21-35), during which the Holy Spirit had ordered the steps of Simeon to the Temple to see the promised Messiah (cf. 2:25-27).

Luke's Gospel notes that John the Baptist announced that Jesus would baptize his followers with the Holy Spirit and fire (3:16) which is an indication of ushering us into the era of the Holy Spirit. Luke gives a similar account of the role of the Holy Spirit in Jesus' baptism (cf. 3:21-22) as the other synoptic Gospels. However, the Holy Spirit also empowers Jesus and led Him into the wilderness (cf. 4:1-2) to face His temptation and to carry out his ministry (cf. 4:14; cf. 4:18).).

Moreover, Luke stresses that Jesus did not only go into the wilderness "led by the Spirit", but that he goes there "full of the Holy Spirit" (4: 1) which no doubt, aided His victory over the tempter. According to Luke, Jesus undertakes his mission "in the power of the Spirit" (4:14). In the synagogue at Nazareth, when he officially begins his mission, Jesus appropriated the prophecy of Isaiah by applying it to Himself (cf. 61:12): "The Spirit of the Lord is upon me because he has anointed me to preach good news to the poor" (4:18)

The Gospel of John

The Gospel of John takes a completely different approach in discussing the Holy Spirit. According to John, the Father sends the Holy Spirit at the Son's request (cf. 14:16). He also notes that the Father sends the Spirit in the name of Jesus (cf. 14:26).

Furthermore, John holds that Jesus sends the Holy Spirit from the Father to provide spiritual help to His followers in His absence (cf. 15:26; 16:7). That is to mean that the Spirit proceeds from the Father (cf. 15:26). John presents the Holy Spirit as taking permanent residence in humanity as alluded in the baptism of Jesus (cf. 1:32-33).

According to him, the Holy Spirit is the believer's permanent possession (cf. 14:16). While Unbelievers cannot perceive the Holy Spirit, a believer is intimately joined with Him (cf. 14:17). In this Gospel, we find the more detailed teaching of Jesus concerning the Holy Spirit as can be found in chapter 14-16.

In John's Gospel, you find a rundown of the functions of the Holy Spirit which includes; our "Comforter" otherwise translated as "Helper" or "Counselor" (cf. 14:16; 14:26; 15:26). He is the "Spirit of truth" (cf. 14:17; 15:26; 16:13).And it is He who guides believers into the truth concerning all things (cf. 14:25-26; 16:12-13); and revealing things to come (cf. 16:13).

Thus, the Spirit will not bring new revelations but will guide believers into a deeper penetration of the truth revealed by Jesus. He aids the disciples of Jesus to come to the remembrance of His words. (cf.14:25-26); thereby, testifying about Jesus (cf. 15:26); It is He who enables believers to witness (cf. 15:27); speaking on behalf of Jesus, and brings glory to Him (16:13-15); The Holy Spirit convinces the world of sin, of righteousness and judgment (cf. 16:8-11). The basic sin which the Paraclete will make known is not to have professed faith in Christ.

The justice referred to is that which the Father gave his crucified Son by glorifying him in the Resurrection and Ascension into heaven. While the judgment referred to in this context, consists in the revealing of the sin of those who are dominated by the prince of this world, Satan (cf. Jn 16:11) and rejected Christ With his inner assistance, the Holy Spirit is, therefore, the defender and supporter of Christ's cause, the One who leads the minds and hearts of disciples to full acceptance of the 'truth' of Jesus.

The Holy Spirit in the Acts of the Apostles

In the Acts of the Apostles, we find several accounts of baptism, impartation/laying on of hands, infilling, role, power, and works of the Holy Spirit.

The book of Acts establishes the pattern that the Holy Spirit is imparted to those who believers at the time of their conversion. This pattern is reinforced in several ways. The imparting of the Holy Spirit to believers was foretold by Jesus before His ascension, a fact that Luke was careful to note (cf. Acts 1:4-5: "you will be baptized with the Holy Spirit"). This promise was fulfilled on Pentecost day (cf. 2:1-4). Through the power of the Spirit, "they were all filled with the Holy Spirit and began to speak in other languages" (2:4). Peter interpreted this phenomenon as the fulfillment of Joel chapter 2:28-32 (2:16-21).

Since after the Pentecost, it became like a norm that believers receive the Holy Spirit at the time of their conversion/baptism. On Pentecost day Peter had identified the reception of the Holy Spirit as a consequence of salvation (cf. 2:37-39). The Holy Spirit is subsequently referred to by the apostles as God's gift to those who obey Him. That is, by trusting Christ for salvation (cf. 5:32). And He is given freely by God and not for sale. To communicate this notion, Peter had to confront Simon the sorcerer to make it clear that the Holy Spirit is a gift given freely to believers (cf. 8:18-24).

Impartation/Laying on of Hands

Those who came to faith in the Samaritan revival did not experience the baptism of the Spirit immediately. The conversion of the first Gentiles in Cornelius's home was accompanied by the falling of the Holy Spirit (cf. 10:44-48). Peter later reflected on this event, equating it with what occurred to the Jewish believers on the Day of Pentecost (cf. 11:15-18; 15:7-9). In the Acts of the Apostles, we can see clearly that some believers did receive the Holy Spirit through impartation as exemplified through the laying on of Peter and John's hands (cf. 8:12, 14-17). We also notice that Saul received the Spirit through the mediation of Ananias three days after he was converted divinely (cf. 9:17).

The author of the Acts of the Apostle equally presents an analogy of a puzzling impartation of the Spirit on the disciples of John the Baptist (cf. 19:1-6). According to him, these men professed to have believed and had been baptized (baptism of John the Baptist) but did not know the Spirit. From the text, it is obvious that they had to profess faith in Jesus Christ and after trusting in Christ and being baptized, they received the Holy Spirit through the imposition of Paul's hands. It appears that the early Church had used the expression 'baptism in the name of Jesus' in order to distinguish the Christian Baptism from the baptism of John and many other baptisms of the Jewish and Gentile religions at that time.

Many More Roles the Holy Spirit Plays

The relationship of the Church with the Spirit is of great importance. This is perhaps nowhere more clearly portrayed than in the story of Ananias and Sapphira, who died because of their irreverence toward the Spirit (cf. 5:1-11). For the most part, however, the early church leaned heavily on the Spirit's direction and empowerment.

The Jerusalem church considered Spirit-filling to be so important that it required it of leaders who would perform seemingly insignificant tasks (cf. 6:2-6). It designated Barnabas, a Spirit-filled man, to journey to Antioch on its behalf (cf.11:22-24). Its leaders sought the Spirit's wisdom in making resolutions that would affect the Christian world of their day (cf. 15:28-29).

The church at Antioch responded to the Spirit's instruction to commission Barnabas and Saul for missionary service (cf. 13:1-4). And Paul recognized the Spirit's role in appointing church leaders in Ephesus (cf. 20:28). He also made tentative plans in the Spirit that he sought the Spirit's direction for his life (cf.19:21).

The Infilling of the Holy Spirit

The book of Acts illustrates that the Holy Spirit works his will by filling believers with His presence as well as with power. The lesson for us today is that Christians should seek to be filled with the Spirit on a continual basis because we are nothing without Him. According to the author of Acts of the Apostles, when Peter was filled with the Holy Spirit, he boldly proclaimed Jesus as Christ to the Jewish leaders (cf. 4:8ff). When Paul was filled with the Spirit, he confronted a sorcerer who was hindering the cause of evangelization (cf. 13:9ff).

The early church recognized the importance of designating faithful, Spirit-filled men to carry out the Lord's work. The Jerusalem church refused to delegate food distribution to men who were less than Spirit-filled and wise (cf. 6:2-6). Also, He selected Barnabas as its representative to Antioch because of his spirituality (cf. 11:22-24). The infilling of the Holy Spirit is associated with joy, and the disciples experienced it even in the face of persecution (cf.13:50-52).

The early church prayed for the infilling of the Holy Spirit, to be enabled to represent the Lord boldly before the world (cf. 4:29-31). You too can pray for an infilling of the Holy Spirit to standout in your calling.

Holy Spirit Our Source of Spiritual Power

The Acts of the Apostles shows that the Holy Spirit leads and empowers the church for growth and service. The success of the Church is essentially connected to her relationship with the Spirit. We avail ourselves of the Spirit's power by walking in Him. By walking in Him, we suppress the works of the flesh and produce the fruit of the Spirit (cf. Gal5:16-25; cf. Eph 5:9; Rom 14:17). 'Walking' here suggests continuing progress in a believer's life in time and in a chosen direction.

The author of Acts of the Apostles presents the Holy Spirit as the Source of spiritual power (cf. 1:8). He also attributed the success of Jesus in His earthly ministry in training the apostles and performing healings to the work of the Spirit (cf.1:2; 10:38). However, the earthly work of Christ serves as a model of ministry which was led and empowered by the Holy Spirit.

The Holy Spirit led and enabled the early Christians to witness boldly on behalf of Jesus (cf. 4:8ff; 5:30-32). Driven by the Spirit, Paul witnessed to the Corinthian Jews concerning the identity of Jesus as Messiah (cf. 18:5). The Spirit empowered Stephen's message to his fellow Jews, forcing them to decide for or against Christ (cf. 6:8-10). Through the Spirit, Paul confronted Elymas the sorcerer's deceitful ways (cf.13:9ff).

Works of the Holy Spirit in the Early Church

In the Acts of the Apostles, the Holy Spirit is presented as the overseer of every aspect of the church's advancement in the first century. The author specifically names Him as the Agent behind the growth of the Church's (cf. 9:31). It was the Holy Spirit who directed Philip to witness to the Ethiopian eunuch (cf. 8:29ff). According to the author, He transported Philip from the desert to Azotus so he could engage in an evangelizing mission (cf. 8:39-40).

It was He who directed Peter to accompany men to Cornelius's house, leading to the inclusion of Gentiles in the Church (cf. 10:19-20; 11:12). The Holy Spirit revealed to a prophet named Agabus that a famine was imminent, thereby enabling the Antioch Church to send some relief material to Jerusalem (cf. 11:27-30). It was He who prevented Paul and his companions from following their own plans to evangelize in particular regions they chose (cf.16:6-7) and to protect Paul, He warned him of imminent dangers of going to Jerusalem (cf. 20:22-23; 21:4, 10-11).

The epistles and Revelation gives the Holy Spirit, a prominent place as He is mentioned in several references. From the references, it is clear that the Spirit plays a major role in the execution of the salvation plan of God. He is presented as the Mediator of Christ's sacrifice to God for the sins of humanity (cf. Heb 9:13-14).

You would also notice that the Spirit is the 'Principal-Agent' of conversion as such, He is active in communicating the gospel message to the unsaved (cf. 1 Thess. 1:5; 1 Pet 1:12). It is He who gives us the knowledge concerning the identity of Jesus Christ as Son of God Almighty (cf.1 Jn. 5:5-9).

The author of the book of Revelation presents Him as the one who joins the Church, the Bride of Christ in inviting the lost ones to come to Jesus (cf. Rev22:17). According to Paul, the Holy Spirit is the Source of life (cf. 2 Cor. 3:6). And to those who accept and profess faith in Christ Jesus, He imparts that life (cf. Gal 3:13-14). Paul further notes that being the "the Spirit of grace," whenever Christ's atoning sacrifice is rejected, He is offended (cf. Heb 10:29).

Possession of the Spirit is thus a telltale sign of genuine faith (cf. Rom 8:9; 8:15; Jude 17-19). Paul also holds that our body is the temple of the Holy Spirit, where He inhabits (cf. 1 Cor6:19-20). The indwelling of the Spirit in believers' hearts guarantees future redemption and also constitutes a seal (cf. Rom 8:9-11; 8:23; 2 Cor. 1:22; 5:5; Eph 1:13-14; 4:30).

The Holy Spirit accompanies believers as they proclaim the gospel message (cf. 1 Pet 1:12). Peter attributes the whole of Old Testament prophecy to the working of the Holy Spirit (cf. 2 Pet 1:20-21). Particularly, he credits the Spirit with revealing Messianic prophecies to the prophets (cf. 1 Pet 1:10-11). The information contained in the book of Revelation came to John by the Holy Spirit (cf. Rev 1:10; 4:2; 14:13; 17:3; 21:10).

Paul teaches that the Spirit is not an abstract or a thing but a Person who likes everyone else can be grieved (cf. Eph 4:30) and quenched (cf. 1 Thess. 5:19). He can be loved as well as related with (cf. 2 Cor. 13:14; Phil 2:1). More so, Paul holds that the Spirit plays a great role in mediating believers' prayer and worship (cf. Eph 6:18; Phil 3:3 Jude 20-21).

He also mediates in our access to God the Father by the death of Christ (cf. Eph 2:18). He even intercedes on our behalf in groans that words cannot express so that God's will may be done in our lives (cf. Rom 8:26-27). It is the Holy Spirit that nurtures our relationship with the Father by affirming our identity as His children continually (cf. Rom 8:15-17; Gal 4:6-7).

How to Receive the Holy Spirit

Believers receive the Spirit by exercising faith in God's message, not by performing the works of the law. The ministry of the new covenant is the ministry of the Spirit (cf. 2Cor 3:4-6). The Spirit is given to those who turn to the Lord through the preaching of the gospel (12-17). Interestingly, it is the Spirit who empowers preachers to share the message of Christ, so that the ministry is carried out, in a sense, by the Spirit Himself (1-3, 18). As the

'Principal-Agent' of conversion, He convicts people of their sin and aids them to be baptized so as to receive Him.

Operations of the Holy Spirit

Paul notes that the Holy Spirit empowers believers to live above the sinful habits of the flesh thereby, overcoming sinful living (cf. Rom8:3-6, 12-13). This is made possible when a believer commends himself or herself to be filled with the Spirit (cf. Eph 5:18). The Spirit fills you with wisdom and discernment of God's will (v 17).

The Holy Spirit enlightens and prompts our consciences to bring about assurance of righteous living (cf. Rom 9:1-2). By implication, He also convicts us when we are in sin to shun sinful acts. He is also the source of inner strength for all believers (cf. Eph. 3:16).

The Holy Spirit concerns Himself with the sanctification of the Church. He serves as a unifier among Christians of diverse backgrounds and personalities (cf. Eph4:1-4). We must endeavor to live out the reality of our oneness by maintaining visible and valuable unity among brothers and sisters in Christ (v 3). This life is made practicable through the grace of patience and humility (1-2).

According to Paul, the Holy Spirit animates believers and gives them every necessary spiritual gift for the building up of the Church, the body of Christ (cf. 1 Cor. 12:4-13). Thereby making this temple, befitting dwelling place for God (cf. Eph 2:19-22).

Weapon of Warfare
He grants believers spiritual armor with which (cf. Eph 6:10ff). One of the elements of this armor, God's Word, is referred to as the Spirit's sword (cf. Eph 6:17). From this, we may infer that the Spirit carries out warfare on our behalf. The Revealer of Mysteries

The Spirit revealed the mystery of the Church to apostles and prophets who would serve as the church's foundation (cf. Eph 3:5-7; cf. 2:20). Furthermore, the Holy Spirit calls men to the sacred trust of administering His Word (cf. 2 Tim 1:14; cf. 1 Tim 6:20).

Empowerment for Ministry is impossible outside the context of the working of the Spirit. The Spirit directs every aspect of believers' service to God, one another, and the world.

The preaching of the early church was carried out "by the Holy Spirit sent from heaven" (1 Pet 1:12). Paul carried out the entirety of his ministry "by the Holy Spirit" (cf. 2 Cor. 6:6). Paul encourages Timothy to keep the ministry that had been entrusted to him by the Holy Spirit (cf. 2 Tim 1:14).

The salvation message of Christ's apostles was reinforced by the Holy Spirit through miracles and spiritual gifts (cf. Heb 2:3-4). The Spirit gives a variety of gifts to believers for the benefit of the church. These are distributed according to His sovereign will (cf. 1 Cor. 12:4-11). The Holy Spirit empowered Paul's speech and actions so that his ministry was fruitful from Jerusalem to Illyricum.

The Spirit's manifestation included both supernatural phenomena and the power of spiritual persuasion (cf.

Rom 15:18-19). The Spirit made Paul's ministry in Corinth useful. He did not approach the Corinthians with his own rhetorical devices, but with the power of God (cf. 1 Cor. 2:4-5). Paul's ministry of the gospel to the Thessalonians was no mere speech communication. It was carried out with the power of the Holy Spirit (Cf. 1 Thess. 1:5).

Spiritual Growth

One of the main essences of the coming of the Holy Spirit is to help believers become as it were, 'another Christ,' having all the spiritual powers that Jesus had during His earthly existence. However, His most predominant role on earth is that of enabling Christians to achieve spiritual growth. It is true that spiritual growth is a work of the Spirit brought about by faith and not works (cf. Gal 3:2-5). But we should not think that we have no responsibility in the matter. It is, however, our duty according to Paul; we are expected to sow to the Spirit thereby making provisions for our spiritual growth and health (cf. Gal 6:7-8

CHAPTER FIVE

GIFTS, OPERATION AND MANAGEMENT

Gifts of the Holy Spirit of God

In our time, it appears there is much controversy regarding the gifts of the Holy Spirit (which we could term Spiritual Gifts), especially with regards to the Charismatic gifts. No doubt as soon as the gift of the Holy Spirit is mentioned, what quickly comes to mind are the Charismatic gifts.

In recent times, not so much is said of the Sanctifying gifts. Greater emphasis is placed on the Charismatic gifts. Even with regards to the Charismatic gifts, we have to understand that according to the Scriptures, God gives certain gifts to humanity at certain points in history for obvious reasons. In the Old Testament era, for instance, some of the gifts were given for definite tasks. As such, some of the gifts given to the church in its early days were not intended to continue indefinitely.

You will agree with me that in our time, we are witnessing a rising tide of sorts of teaching that is connected with Pentecostalism and charismaticism" these days. We need to ask if this is truly God's work and purpose. And if it does fit the teaching of His Word?"

The Catholic Church teaches that there are special graces, also called charisms after the Greek term used by St. Paul and meaning 'favor,' 'gratuitous gift,' 'benefit. Whatever their character sometimes it is extraordinary, such as the gift of miracles or tongues. Charismatic gifts are oriented towards the common good of the Church. All are at the service of charity which builds up the Church (CCC. 2003).

The time has come when we have to clearly define what we believe and stand by it with earnest conviction. We can only influence a younger generation for the truth if we are fully convinced of it ourselves. A lack of knowledge in this area of the gifts of the Holy Spirit has resulted in confusion among some believers who do not know what they should believe or where they should stand. We hope this consideration will be helpful to some in this area. Our object is to consider the various gifts of the Holy Spirit, their operations and how they can be managed to fulfill the intention of the giver. However, to ensure that no stone is left unturned, let us consider the categories of gifts.

CATEGORIES OF GIFTS

We need to understand first of that gift varies. And there are two broad categories of gifts; Motivational or Natural Gifts, and Spiritual or Supernatural Gifts. Distinguishing these categories of gifts is pertinent. Motivational Gifts

(Natural Abilities/Talents) and Spiritual Gifts as can be seen in Romans 12:6-8. Though our main concern in this book is the spiritual gifts, and we cannot properly understand the Spiritual Gifts unless a clear distinction is made of these gifts. There are mainly three broad categories of Spiritual Gifts: Motivational or Natural Gifts; Sanctifying Gifts and Charismatic Gifts. Let us discuss this various categories of gifts however, paying more attention to the Charismatic Gifts that the Holy Spirit gives.

MOTIVATIONAL OR NATURAL GIFTS

Motivational Gifts are talents/abilities which God gives to a person from the very moment of his or her conception in the womb. These talents are called gifts because they are freely given to the one who has it by God to enable him, or her contribute positively to our society and bring glory to Him as we utilize them. The gifts help us to develop our personalities, character, and often our vocations. These are gifts that in some measure are present in each of us, even though one may be more prevalent than another.

A Christian may use a natural ability that the Lord can give for the growth of the Church, His honor and glory. However, these gifts are different from spiritual gifts. One way to distinguish a natural ability from a spiritual gift is to realize that a Natural Ability/Talent a believer might have is one that an unsaved person might also possess. But a spiritual gift can only be possessed by a person who is 'born again' (Baptized), the Holy Spirit imparts such gifts, like the "gift of singing" or a "gift of music" or other abilities of that nature. Even an ability to speak publicly can be mistaken for a spiritual gift. One may have an ability linked with his physical makeup in any area of life, but it is not a spiritual gift. No unbaptized person has any of the spiritual gifts spoken of in the Scriptures. Every mention of spiritual gift or instruction about its exercise is directed entirely toward those who are born again.

THE CATEGORIES OF SPIRITUAL GIFTS

Two major categories of Spiritual Gifts may be distinguished; Sanctifying Gifts which refers to the graces given for personal sanctification and Charismatic Gifts which has to do with extraordinary graces given to individual Christians for the good of others. According to Mark Shea, Confirmation is ordered toward friendship with God and mission to the world. Therefore, when you are confirmed, the Holy Spirit pours out on you two kinds of gifts sanctifying and charismatic gifts reflecting those twin purposes of God.

THE SANCTIFYING GIFTS

In the teaching of the Catholic Church, seven gifts of the Holy Spirit are recognized as the Sanctifying gifts; a listing of these gifts is found in Isaiah 11:2-3. According to Scott P. Richert, these sanctifying gifts of the Holy Spirit are fully present in Jesus Christ, but all Christians who are in a state of grace also have them.

We receive these graces when we are infused with sanctifying grace, the life of God within us as the Sanctifying gifts are an endowment to which every baptized Christian can lay claim from his earliest childhood. They are our heritage. These gifts which we receive in the sacraments and develop through experience are formidable to the successful conduct of the Christian life. They do not appear spontaneously or out of nowhere but, they emerge gradually as the fruit of virtuous living. Because they are our spiritual weaponry for the spiritual warfare of everyday life, they are taken from us by the Spirit for they are perpetually needed as long as we are fighting the good fight.

The Sanctifying gifts are designed to be used in the world for the purpose of transforming that world for Christ. Isaiah 11 vividly portrays what these gifts are to be used to do what one is called to do in one's own time and place, advancing the kingdom of God. The specific, personal details of that call do not come into focus until one has realized his minimal, unpalatable place in the line-up of things (fear of the Lord), accepted one's role as a member of God's family (piety), and acquired the habit of following the Father's specific directions for living a moral life (knowledge).

This familiarity with God breeds the strength and courage needed to confront the evil that one inevitably encounters in one's life (fortitude) and the cunning to nimbly shift one's strategies to match even anticipate the many machinations of the Enemy (counsel). The more one engages in such "spiritual battles," the more one knows how such skirmishes connects to the big picture that is God's master plan for establishing his reign in this fallen world (understanding) and the more confident, and successful one becomes in the conduct of his particular vocation (wisdom).

Traditional Explanation of the Sanctifying Gifts

As considered in the Catholic Answers Magazine, the seven gifts of the Holy Spirit are heroic character traits that Jesus Christ alone possesses in their fullness, and he freely shares same with believers. These traits are deposited in every Christian as a permanent endowment at baptism, and they are nurtured through the practice of the seven virtues and sealed in the sacrament of confirmation. They are also known as the sanctifying gifts of the Spirit, because they serve the purpose of rendering their recipients docile to the leadings of the Holy Spirit in their lives, thereby helping them to grow daily in holiness and making them fit to see God face to face. Let us consider the nature of these gifts.

The nature of the Sanctifying Gifts has been a subject of debated by theologians since the mid-second century, the standard interpretation has been the one that St. Thomas Aquinas worked out in the thirteenth century in his Summa Theologiae. Let us consider the nature of each of the seven gifts.

Nature of the Sanctifying Gifts

Wisdom - This is an understanding in our inner being, which enables us to see things from God's viewpoint. It helps us to develop the ability to make judgments about everything in our lives by a deep, one to one union with the Lord and his abiding love. Thomas Aquinas in his Summa Theologiae notes that it is both the knowledge of and the judgment about divine things as well as the ability to judge and direct human affairs according to divine truth.

Understanding –This is the enlightenment of our minds and hearts with the divine truth so that we can understand the mysteries of the Lord. This gift enables us to see the Lord more deeply. According to Aquinas, it is penetrating insight into the very heart of things, especially those higher truths we need are for our eternal salvation, in effect, the ability to see God. It also illuminates the Holy Scriptures as we read them and gives us knowledge of God and his ways. Signs of this gift are new insight into the Scriptures, increased depth in prayer, and a renewed appreciation of the sacraments.

Counsel (Right Judgment) – Is the ability to receive and give good advice. It enables us to make a Spirit aided decisions in practical life situations in all spheres of our existence. According to Aquinas, it allows a man to be directed by God in matters necessary for his salvation. Sometimes we experience it in the sacrament of Reconciliation. The Holy Spirit helps us to discern good from evil, or right from wrong. We grow in this gift by humbling ourselves to seek help from others when faced with a difficult situation.

Fortitude (Courage / Strength / Zeal) – It enables us to face with strength the trials and dangers we encounter in our Christian life. It empowers us to choose consistently the right way to live in spite of disappointments and difficulties. Aquinas holds that it is firmness of the mind in doing good and in avoiding evil, especially when it is practically difficult to do so or dangerous, and the confidence to overcome all obstacles, even deadly ones, by the assurance of everlasting life.

Knowledge – Means having a deep trust and sureness about the Lord and knowing the truths of Christian revelation. According to Aquinas, it is the ability to judge correctly in all matters of faith and right action, to never wander from the straight path of justice. This gift of the Holy Spirit produces in us a deep trust in the Lord. We grow in the gift of knowledge through the daily study of the scriptures and the teachings of the Church.

Piety (Love) – St Paul in his letter to the Romans (8:15) called it the "spirit of adoption" which produces in us a loving and worshipful consciousness of God as our Father.

Aquinas notes that it is principally, revering God with filial affection, paying worship and duty to God, paying due duty to all men on account of their relationship to God, and honoring the saints and not contradicting Scripture. The Latin word pietas denote the reverence that we give to our father and our country; and in our case, God is the Father of all, the worship of God is also called piety. Piety helps us to get a true image of God as a merciful, faithful, abounding in steadfast love. It also helps us to see God's holiness reflected in other people and to love them as they are. We grow in piety through the practice of justice, which refers to attitudes of cooperation with authority, truthfulness, friendliness, and humility.

Fear of the Lord – This may be said to be an attitude of reverence and awe in the presence of God. According to Aquinas, it is "filial" or chaste fear whereby we revere God and avoid separating ourselves from him—as opposed to "servile" fear, whereby we fear punishment. It should not be mistaken with the emotion of fear; that is fear of offending God which is a manifestation of respect and reverence for who God is.

This gift helps us to reverence all life as a reflection of God's life. Fear of the Lord may be seen as the spiritual door which opens us to the full Christian life. (cf. Psalm 111:10; Proverbs 9:10; Psalm 34:12-15). We grow in reverence by praying to God often, by being thankful for God's gifts, and by respecting His name.

These gifts, according to Aquinas, are "instincts," "dispositions," or "habits," which God provide by as a supernatural help to man in the process of his "perfection." They enable man to transcend the limitations of human reason and human nature and participate in the very life of God, as Christ promised (John 14:23). Aquinas insists that they are necessary for man's salvation, which he cannot achieve on his own. They serve to "perfect" the four cardinal virtues of prudence, justice, fortitude, and temperance and the three theological virtues of charity, hope, and faith. But the virtue of charity is the key that unleashes the potential power of the seven gifts, which may lie dormant in the soul after baptism unless so acted upon.

More so, Aquinas holds that because "grace builds upon nature," the seven gifts work closely with the seven virtues as well as with the eight beatitudes and the twelve fruits of the Spirit.

The emergence of these gifts is fostered by the practice of the virtues, which are perfected through exercising the gifts. When the gift is exercised properly, it produces the fruits of the Spirit in the Christian's life which includes: love, peace, patience, joy, kindness, goodness, generosity, faithfulness, modesty, gentleness, self-control, and chastity (Gal. 5:22–23). The goal of this cooperation among virtues, gifts, and fruits is the attainment of the eight-fold state of beatitude described by Christ in the Sermon on the Mount (Matt. 5:3–10).

CHARISMATIC GIFTS

Charismatic gifts are, in contrast, the gifts that we receive to enable us to serve others. They aren't given to build us up but so that we might build up others and bring God's will in our Communities to fruition and renew the face of the earth. For instance, the person with the gift of preaching preaches not to himself, but to edify his or her audience, the giver's money is not there to make him or her overweight but to help the poor person. The one who has the beautiful singing voice exercises it for the ears of others. The charismatic gifts enable us to assist in the process whereby God makes others holy, supplies their needs and heal their wounds. But what matters most is that even when we exercise the Charismatic gifts, we avoid using the gifts to the detriment of our salvation.

The sanctifying gifts are the more essential gifts which God promises that we will receive all of them. In contrast, though everybody gets some sort of charism or charisms because everybody has a God-given mission and s such, needs the tools to carry out that mission, but nobody gets all or even most of the charismatic gifts. Instead, the charisms are, as St. Paul said, distributed throughout the body of Christ so that each member can serve others with their particular gifts. But everybody receives the sanctifying gifts of wisdom, understanding, counsel, fortitude, knowledge, piety and fear of the Lord. Often, in the sacrament of Confirmation we affirm our acceptance of the Charismatic gifts, but often they are not stirred up into activity until we are "baptized in the Holy Spirit."

According to Rev. William G, It is not true that extraordinary charismatic gifts are simply actualizations, putting to work the gifts of the Holy Spirit that all Catholics have. Remember, the special charismatic gifts belong to one category, and the seven Gifts to another. One cannot suppose graces from one side of this divide will actualize those from the other side.

It must be noted that the possession of a Charismatic gift is not an indication of that believer's spirituality. Some make the mistake of equating spirituality with possession of a spiritual gift, especially if that gift is distinguished publicly. The distinction between spiritual gift and spirituality is that the gift is given sovereignly according to the purposes of God while spirituality is dependent on the condition and exercise of the believer.

We see the clearest example of this in the Church in Corinth. (I Cor.1:7). Their gifts resulted from a genuine work of salvation in that the testimony of Christ had been confirmed in them (v.6). I Cor. 12-14 show us that the believers of that assembly had an abundant spiritual gift and were seeking to exercise it (though not in the right way). But they were carnal (I Cor. 3:1) and by their behavior, they were clearly displaying every evidence that they were not spiritual. It is sad, and it can be a big problem for the assembly when there is one who has a spiritual gift, and because of that gift he or she is given or takes a prominent place among the brethren, but he or she is not in a suitable spiritual condition to use it properly. Enormous harm can be done because of this, as such, it is necessary for every believer to seek spiritual fitness for the proper exercise of any gift. We will consider this in detail in subsequent pages. For now, let us consider the Spiritual Gifts in detail.

Whenever we exercise the gifts of the Holy Spirit with careful discernment of spirits and obedience, they are useful for the needs of the Church (cf. LG 12).

We need to know that, the possession of charismatic gifts is not a certainty to prove that anyone who has a gift is in the state of grace. We think of the frightening words of Our Lord Jesus Christ (Mt 7. 22-23) that many will say to me on that day: Lord, Lord, I prophesied in your name, and in your name, cast out demons, and have done many marvels in your name? And then I will admit to them: I never knew you: depart from me you workers of iniquity."

Essence of the Gifts of the Holy Spirit

A spiritual gift is one of the expressions of the Holy Spirit's work through the individual believer. A gift is not just an enabling ability for that person to use according to his desire or power. It is to be used under the guidance and control of the Holy Spirit and for the purposes which God has intended it to be used. That gift is a "manifestation of the Spirit" (I Cor. 12:7), and He purposes to accomplish some essential work through that gift for the blessing of the believers, the building up of the body of Christ, the help and strengthening of the local communities of the Church as well as the evangelization of the lost(Eph. 4: 12-15; 14:24-26

The Gift of the Holy Spirit is not given to an individual believer on merits. It is not because one is better than another child of God that he or she receives a certain gift. These gifts are dispensed according to the infinite knowledge, wisdom, and purpose of God.

The Spirit of God by Himself divides or distributes to everyone individually or in particular according to His will alone. This means it is outside the realm of man's choice or determination altogether. But one might object to this on the grounds of 2Tim.1:6 Where Paul speaks of the gift of God that was in Timothy by the laying on of his hands. It should be noted that if this passage teaches that Timothy received a gift by this means, it was because the Holy Spirit chose to work in that way at that time even as He chose to impart the Holy Spirit to the new Samaritan believers in Acts 1: 8 through Peter's hands.

God gives a spiritual gift to be used for the blessing of others and to further God's purpose of bringing His work in the Church to completion. Those gifts are exercised in

111

evangelization as God works to reach the lost. They are put into use in the Community and other believers to build up the body of Christ by teaching and personal ministry to them. Through these gifts given to men, God's blessing can be displayed and realized. A gift is not exercised privately or toward the believer who receives the gift in the sense of using a gift for his or her benefit. That gift has to be exercised in ministry for the building up of the body. It should be noted that anyone who misuses any of these gifts would be doing so at his or her detriment. No gift is given to be used privately or for personal benefit.

In addition, every gift is intended to be exercised in relation to a local assembly and its functions. We can see from the Scripture that the intent of the Holy Spirit is that the entire gift is to be exercised in relation to the activities and fellowship of the Community. Even the gift of evangelization is an extension of the gospel activity of a Christian Community, Christians were doing when they went everywhere preaching the gospel.

So very often many people ask this important question, "Do I have any gift? What is the gift and how can I know how to put it to use?" Sometimes, some persons get so discouraged so that as a result they do not seek to know what their gift is.

Some may have been told or think that they do not possess a Charismatic gift, but the Scripture we are told that those gifts are given to every believer for mutual profit (I Cor.12:7). That is to say that the Spirit of God gives a unique Charismatic gift depending on the need of the Community. St. Paul offers an illustration of this using the analogy of the human body (12:14-26) he shows that just as every member of the physical body has its unique place and ability corresponding to it, even so, is it true for every believer. This implies that the Holy Spirit equips every believer with gifts so that they can contribute to the well-being and advancement of the assembly where God has placed them.

So how does one ascertain what their spiritual gift is? There is little in the Scripture that would give us a clear answer to this question. It would almost seem that such silence shows that a believer if exercised before the Lord, would have an intuitive understanding of what gift they have received. That is, that the Holy Spirit indwelling each believer can ably work with and toward each one to make that believer know what work He has fitted him or her for. It may be that the believer will recognize a particular inclination toward an aspect of the work needed in the assembly and be able to discern a corresponding ability needed for that work or service.

Possibly one might discern his or her gift by seeking to understand what each gift listed involves, and from that point carefully and prayerfully seek to learn what the Spirit of God has equipped him or her to do. We can encourage believers to exercise themselves in various activities of service for the Lord within their particular spheres, and shortly they will recognize if they are fit for it or not. That is not to say that the God-given ability will be seen in its fully-developed condition; every gift has to be developed in some way by its use, and through that exercise, it will be clearer over time what gift has been given.

In the Old Testament, God usually pointed out those with a gift to others as having been mainly raised up by Him. You would notice in Num.27:15-23 how God pointed out Joshua to Moses concerning leading His people after Moses' death (Deut.34:9). In the same way, God made clear to Moses that He had raised up Bezaleel and Aholiab for the work of the tabernacle (Ex. 31:1,6) as well as other wise-hearted men of the camp of Israel. Could we draw from this the conclusion that men who have spiritual discernment, the elders of an assembly, should be concerned to help younger believers recognize the particular gift God has given them. It will be a healthy condition for a Community if younger believers have confidence in older believers so that they could freely express them and have an assurance that they could receive spiritual counsel in these things. We can be sure that if there is a spiritual exercise on the part of a believer to know what gift God has given, coupled with a willingness to fulfill the service connected with that gift, there will be an understanding communicated to him. Perhaps challenge lies in the fact that in our busy lives we don't spend the time waiting on God and earnestly seeking His will as we should so that we might know clearly from Him what` spiritual enablement He has endowed us with.

Exercise of Charismatic Gift

There is a great need for every believer to understand how gifts are to be exercised in the Church. There should be room for the exercise of every scriptural gift in an assembly. Properly, one of the criticisms of the practices of Christendom is that there is no room or opportunity for believers to exercise the gifts God has given them. Certainly, this is a form of "quenching the Spirit" (I Thess. 5:19) and is the prominent sin against the Holy Spirit today.

The best portion that tells us how spiritual gifts are to be exercised is in I Cor.12-14. Briefly, let us observe the following principles that are given us in that section.

Gifts are to be exercised harmoniously, in fellowship with others, working together with the saints of that assembly (I Cor.12:14-17). It is an abnormal condition in anybody when the members don't function together for the good of the entire body; in that case, we call it a disease. Every member with its unique ability works in perfect harmony with others who are also a part of that body. The assembly is the Body of Christ, and it is to function as a body in this aspect of having members working in harmony together. What a blessing when this is the case! Then we see that there is not to be any envy of others or disparaging or belittling of others in the assembly as they exercise themselves for God and His glory. All gifts are important, and it seems that the ones that are not seen are the more important ones. It is of the flesh when we fail to appreciate the different aspects of service which every saint is seeking to contribute to the well-being of the assembly. If we recognize that gifts are given sovereignly by the Spirit of God (1 Cor. 12:4-7, 11), we will appreciate everyone who has been so equipped by God for the work He has given them. That principle lies on the surface of 1

Cor. 12:18-26. God has set the members in the body, placing them where He wills so that all might be tempered together, that there might not be any schism in the body. All suffer if one suffers; all rejoice if one rejoices. May our Lord Jesus Christ give us the grace to express our appreciation freely for the helpful contribution of every saint in the assembly!

Gifts should be exercised with an earnest desire that God would raise up in the Community the "better gifts" (1`Cor. 12:31). No doubt in the context of this passage, he is referring to the gifts that the Corinthian believers were not emphasizing, and instead of the gifts such as tongues, they should have been seeking the gifts that would edify the assembly. But cannot we also have an exercise before the Lord so that we can discern when there is a need because of the lack of gift that is required? For example, when there is a lack of sound teaching because there are no teachers in that assembly, it should cause the saints to pray earnestly that God would raise up such gift in the assembly, however, He might choose to do it.

There are times when gifts are lacking in an assembly and the assembly suffers because of that lack. That lack may be due to various reasons, some of which may be that there are believers in fellowship in that assembly who are not exercising the gift God has given them. Perhaps, also, there are those whom God intended to place (12:18) in that assembly, but for one reason or another they never came into that assembly or are no longer there. Whatever the reason, we need the discernment and exercise to pray that whatever gift may be needed in the assembly might be given, so that the assembly might prosper.

St. Paul unmistakably tells us that all gifts are to be exercised in love (cf. 1 Cor. 13). This is the ingredient that makes the assembly function smoothly, it is the 'oil' that enables the 'machinery' to work together as it should. More than all else that includes love for the Lord, then love for all those who will be affected by that service.

Evidently, this was lacking in Corinth (as is often the case). Concerning the exercise of the gifted men in Eph.4, they are exhorted to speak "the truth in love" (Eph. 4:15) so that the body might make increase of itself for the edifying of itself in love (cf. Eph. 4:16). We all know of times when the exercise of gift has not been controlled by love for the saints, the assembly, or the Lord, and much harm can be and has been the result.

All gifts are to be exercised so that the assembly might be edified, or built up. That is the teaching of I Cor.14. Many gifts, including speaking in tongues, were being exercised in the assembly in Corinth then, but the exercise of them under certain circumstances was futile for there was no blessing imparted to the hearers. We should always keep this before us when we are exercising a gift God has given.

The object of using it or doing anything for God is that the result of that exercise might be the blessing of the saints, their building up and strengthening, and also that the lost might be reached. Ultimately its purpose is that God might be glorified and Christ exalted. Reasons stemming only from selfish desires, desires for prominence or place, or that show a disregard for the effect that would come from that exercise should be judged and avoided.

We would suggest from 14:26 that gift is to be the result of personal exercise with regard to the Community. All believers should come prepared to participate in the manner for which God has enabled them. We must keep in mind that praying, expressing worship, and some other aspects of assembly gathering do not depend on gift, but there are other functions listed here that do. Proper function of an assembly depends on every believer being exercised to uphold the responsibility that the Lord has entrusted to them. Fellowship in an assembly is a privilege that brings with it a corresponding responsibility.

A gift is exercised under the control of the believer, guided by the Spirit of God and in subjection to other brethren (1 Cor. 14:29-33). What was being practiced in Corinth was an outrage against the orderly Spirit-guided exercise of spiritual gift. We are not free to simply let our imagination run loose and think that we can do whatever we like without any control. The closing principle of the chapter is that scriptural order is to be maintained (1 Cor. 14:34-40). To have a gift is excellent but it is to be exercised in the sphere God has given the recipient. In the same way, all brethren must seek to maintain the order the

CHARISMATIC GIFTS AND THEIR DEFINITION

Word of Wisdom (1Cor 12:8)

This gift is distinct from natural wisdom or even the Sanctifying gift of Wisdom. It is one of the Charismatic gifts of the Holy Spirit which enables the bearer to give an overruling counsel or advice which gives a lasting solution in a given situation and helps to solve a problem in the community.

Word of Knowledge (1 Cor. 12:8)

This gift is a Charismatic gift, and it is distinct from natural knowledge and the Sanctifying gift of Knowledge. It gives its bearer the supernatural ability to know a thing; situation or an event/occurrence without prior knowledge of same.

Gift of Faith (1 Cor. 12:8-10)

This refers to that strong or special faith distinguished from the "saving" and "normal" Christian faith. This Faith disposes you to firmly be persuaded of God's power and promises to accomplish His will and display such a confidence in Him and His Word that circumstances and obstacles do not shake that conviction until there is a manifestation.

Discernment of Spirit (1 Cor. 12:10)

This gift gives its bearer the supernatural ability to be able to distinguish clearly truth from error by judging whether the behavior or teaching is from God, Satan, human error, or human power as well as to identify the spirit that is operating in a given circumstance or situation.

Gift of Tongues: (1 Cor. 12:10; 14:27-28)

This is a supernatural ability to speak in a particular language not previously learned so that the community is edified and unbelievers can hear God's message in their language and be ministered to. St. Paul seems to have distinguished between the public use of the gift which must always be interpreted and the private use which was for the spiritual strengthening of oneself.

Interpretation of Tongues (1 Cor. 12:10; 14:27-28)

This refers to a supernatural ability to translate a message spoken in tongues.

Working of Miracles (1 Cor. 12:10, 28)

This gift is one that enables its bearer to supernaturally perform mighty deeds which witnesses acknowledge to be a miracle, that is, of supernatural origin and means.

Gift of Healing Cor. 12:9, 28, 30

The bearer of this gift becomes a means through which God makes people whole either physically, spiritually, emotionally, or mentally. The healing may be instantly or gradual

Gifts of Prophecy (Rom 12:6; 1 Cor. 12:10; Eph. 4:11)

The gift of prophecy (Greek Word: prophetes - the forth-telling of the will of God; 'pro'-forth; 'phemi'-to speak) is a supernatural ability to speak forth the message of God to His people. This gift is distinct from the gift of teaching as defined.

Prophet (1 Cor. 12:28; 14:3; Eph. 4:11)

This is one of the gifts that is greatly misused in our time. The office of prophet is to equip believers for the work of service through exhortation, consolation, and edification, (1 Corinthians 12:28; 1 Corinthians 14:3 Ephesians 4:11). One who has this gift usually exercises or manifests the gift of Prophecy which enables the prophet to report something that spontaneously brings to his or her mind.

Evangelization (Eph. 4:11)

The gift of evangelization enables its bearer by a supernatural ability to be a messenger of the Gospel (Greek Word: euaggelistes - preacher of the gospel; eu-well, Angelos-message - messenger of good), which is literally a messenger of the Good News.

Exhortation (Rom. 12:8)

The gift of exhortation (Greek Word: paraklesis - calling to one's side), enables the one who receives it to have a supernatural ability to comfort, give consolation, counsel and a worthwhile words of encouragement to help someone in need them to be all God wants them to be

125

Leadership (Rom 12:8)

The gift of leadership is an Administrative gift which gives its bearer a supernatural ability to be at the forefront or showing direction, motivating and caring for those you lead to accomplish their giving goals in the Body of Christ.

Pastor (Eph. 4:11)

This gift falls under the category/group of Administrative Gifts, it disposes its bearer with grace to be responsible for spiritually caring for, protecting, guiding, and feeding a group of believers entrusted to his or her care.

Administration (1 Cor. 12:28)

The gift of administration (Greek Word: kubernesis - to steer, guide, helmsmen) is a gift which gives its bearer the supernatural ability to steer the body toward the accomplishment of God-given goals and directives through planning, organizing, and supervising others.

Apostle (Eph. 4:11; 1 Cor. 12:28)

This is one of the hierarchical gifts (Greek Word: Apostolos -'apo'-from 'Stello'-send; one sent forth). One who is sent forth to new frontiers with the gospel divinely enabled to provide leadership over Church Communities and exercise authority over spiritual matters that pertain to the Body of Christ.

Service/Stewardship (Rom 12:7)

The gift of stewardship or service (Greek Word: Diakonia - deacon, attendant 'diako'-to run errands) is a supernatural gift that dispenses the necessary grace to its bearer to identify undone tasks in the community of God's people, however menial, and to use available resources to get the job done.

Teaching Gift: Rom. 12:7; 1 Cor. 12:28; Eph. 4:11

This gift enables its bearer to instruct others in the Bible, Faith, and Morals logically and systematically thereby communicate pertinent information for true understanding and spiritual growth.

Giving: Those who receive this gift share their possessions with others with extraordinary generosity. They go beyond the normal giving, to share whatever material resources you have with liberality and cheerfulness without any condition.

Hospitality/Outreach: 1 Pet. 4:9, 10

The gift of hospitality/outreach (Greek Word: philoxenos - love of strangers; 'Philos'-love; 'Xenos'=stranger) disposes one who receives it to be hospitable to people, even strangers, such that he or she receives same into one's home or church as a means of serving those in need.

Helps or Welfare: 1 Cor. 12:28

This gift comes under the Ministry gifts. It gives its receiver the supernatural enablement to render support or assistance to others in the Community to carry them along. It is someone who gives his or her time, talent, energy and finances to benefit others and advance the Gospel message; a person of faith who knows that God supplies every need, and is willing to put themselves as well as their resources at the service of others in the Community.

Every believer is expected to give to the Lord, to needy brethren, and to others as the Lord directs them. Bearing in mind that all that we have we got from God (I Cor.6:19-20, II Cor.8:5, 9:8-13). That implies that we are only stewards of those possessions with the opportunity to use them for His purposes alone. Notwithstanding, the gift of giving may be a form of this exercise that goes beyond that kind of giving seen in most believers.

One Who Shows Mercy: Rom. 12; Peter 4:8-11

This gift enables its receiver to be sensitive toward those who are suffering, whether physically, mentally, or emotionally. To feel genuine sympathy for their misery; one who is full of; love, compassion, and cares so much for those in need, he or she easily recognizes the pain people experience and tries to bring a solution, healing, and love into action; thereby, helping others to work together in love. Speaking words of compassion more so caring for them with deeds of love to help minister to their condition and needs.

OPERATION OF THE CHARISMATIC GIFTS

St. Paul notes that "To each, the manifestation of the Spirit is given for some benefit." (1 Cor. 12:7) - There are different members, but one BODY all function together.

These gifts are free and are dispensed sovereignly by God upon His people for the good of others. These gifts are supernatural abilities bestowed upon individuals by the Holy Spirit. They are not natural abilities. The Charismatic gifts consist of gifts of Revelation/Insight, gifts of Communication/Utterance, Power/Dynamic gifts and Ministry gifts.

Gifts of Revelation or Insight

Word of Knowledge

The gift of Word of Knowledge is supernatural enablement that gives the bearer a revelation of facts either; past, present, or future which he or she was not informed. This is a supernaturally imparted Word. If we proclaim healing or promise of salvation because of what we have studied, we are presumptuous, not faith-filled. True supernatural knowledge starts with knowing God personally, through Jesus Christ. Jesus and the disciples received many 'words of knowledge' from the Holy Spirit. See John 4:17-27, Matthew 17:27, Mark 5:36-40, Acts 5:1-9, Acts 3:1-10. On Pentecost day, St. Peter manifesting this gift, outlined

God's plan in Jewish history and interpreted for those gathered the recent events of Jesus; death and resurrection and the sending of the Holy Spirit, so many were captivated by his message and accepted the Lordship of Christ.

Word of Wisdom

This gift is a supernatural enablement which reveals God's timing and method of ministry in a given situation. It explains or illuminates a given revelation such as a word of knowledge, discernment of spirit or the communication of revealed prophecy. It is not the same as the wisdom we gain from our experiences in life or intellectual pursuits. We don't have to confuse this gift with the Baptismal or Sanctifying gift of wisdom.

The 'virtue' of wisdom given at Baptism and affirmed at Confirmation is a lifelong gift which increases in us as we yield to those who instruct us on our spiritual journey. But a 'word of wisdom' is a supernatural revelation of God's timing and method of ministry in a given situation. It enables a person to open his or her audience to God's wisdom in handling situation or to react to it, or to silence an opponent. It is the right word in times of opportunity or emergency.

A classic example can be seen in I Kings 3:16. King Solomon manifested it to solve the dispute between the two women who claimed to be the mother of the same baby. In the Gospel of Luke (Luke 18:22), Jesus exercising this gift tells the rich young man who wants to know what to do to enter eternal life li sell all that he had and give the money to the poor, then come and follow him in order for him to gain the kingdom of God. In Matthew 22:21, Jesus silences his opponents when he directs them to "render unto Caesar that which is Caesar's and to God that which is God's." It is usually manifested in a one to one situation, to give counsel or advice. When the need arises, the Lord gives an inspiration regarding what to say to a person that will suit what that person needs to hear at that moment or in a given situation.

It gives its receiver or bearer, a supernatural ability to know or discover if the Holy Spirit is motivating someone or a situation, or their human spirit, an evil spirit or a combination of all is responsible for the action. The discernment of spirits is not an adept ability to read human minds or suspect that something is wrong in the motive of other people. The discernment of spirits is a supernatural gift which disposes its receiver to revelation. This revelation can come through a sensation, a vision, or a specific word. The gift of discernment of spirits is very essential in giving counsel. It has to do with spirits not with men in their natural course of action. It enables one who has it to discover what spirit motivates an individual in a given situation; the Holy Spirit, the human spirit, or an evil spirit. It helps or serves as a defense against deception because it enables one to detect the activity of the evil one.

This gift is significant for every believer especially for leaders of prayer groups because it allows them to discern whether the manifestations at a prayer meeting are from

133

God, from the human spirit or an evil spirit. Every believer needs to discern where the inspiration he or she receives comes from. It is pertinent to bear in mind that one must never rely solely on one's discernment in any situation, but must always seek the discernment of the body of believers. This gift is proof of God's protection for his church. He does not want his people who are bought with the precious blood of Jesus, to become easy prey to the enemy. If one is in the grip of the enemy, God wants to reveal that through this gift so that the person may be set free from such captivity.

Gifts of Communication or Utterance

Tongues

The gift of Tongue is a spontaneously inspired utterance given by the Holy Spirit in which we use our voice according to the Spirit's prompting; to speak or sing in Tongues or to pray in the Spirit. This is what happens if a believer allows the indwelling Spirit to influence the utterance. To pray, to speak or to sing in Tongues is to pray in what could be a human but foreign language to the speaker. That is, he or she has not previously learned it but speaks it so fluently. The language may be current on the earth or one long dead, or it could be any one of countless dialects in the world. Praying in tongues brings inspiration, refreshment, and deliverance (both physically and spiritually). It could also lead to a revival and victory in spiritual warfare against the kingdom of darkness.

Prayer tongue is a unique gift which lasts as long as the believer exercises it and is undoubtedly edifying. Romans 8:26: says that the Spirit prays within you, helping us in our weakness because we are unable to pray as we necessarily ought, but the Spirit himself intercedes for us with sighs too deep for words. The ministerial gift of tongues is distinct from 'speaking' in tongues. In prayer, you pray in tongues, but when you minister to the community in tongues, you speak in tongues. True prayer tongues, you praise God. While the gift of speaking in tongues, while praising God, has as its goal, the release of interpretation, or speaking God's message. Praying in tongues is a permanent gift. Speaking in tongue is a transient gift used only when there is an anointing."

Unlike the other Charismatic gifts, praying in tongues seems to be given to all who desire it, and it need not be followed by interpretation.

According to St. Paul, the gift of tongues is seen to be the "least" of the gifts, though it is often presented as a significant manifestation of the baptism in the Spirit. But it may be said to be the 'gateway' gift to the other gifts of the Spirit. Whenever we humble ourselves in relating with the Lord, so much as to yield to His Holy Spirit within us and speak in tongues, then we open ourselves so much more to surrender to the other gifts in us for the good of the Church. Tongues for the Community which when interpreted equal prophecy are meant primarily to release God's message to the community and must always be followed by an interpretation.

Interpretation of Tongues

The one who manifests this gift is giving the divine enablement to translate what has been spoken in a foreign language so that the hearers can understand the message. If someone speaks in a tongue, there has to be someone to interpret. This can be done by the person who has given the tongue, or it may be given by someone else in the group as influenced by the Giver of the gift. It is the responsibility of the leadership to make sure that no praising, singing, scripture reading, or other prophetic tongue occurs until time has been allowed for the interpretation. This is necessary to avoid confusion in the Community.

Interpretation of tongues may come in a variety of ways, similar to the length and style of the tongue spoken; or it may be completely different, expressed in longer or shorter words, as a vision, a sense, an inspired thought or a symbol in pictures. The person with the interpretation may receive it as if the person speaking in tongues were talking to them in their native language, or it may just be a phrase or a word that comes as the individual is speaking in tongues. The necessary ingredient for bringing forth a message in tongues or an interpretation is the willingness to trust God. This gift, like all the manifestations or gifts of the Holy Spirit, needs to be encouraged and used in our time.

Prophecy

This may be said to be a supernatural communication from God to an individual or a group of believers. It is an ability given by the Spirit to anyone open to bringing forth a message full of love to their brothers and sisters in Christ to promote the spiritual growth and development of the Community. Prophecy builds up, encourages, exhorts and consoles, it may also come as warnings to draw us closer to God. It may stir up a response from the audience such as joy, peace of mind, tranquility, unusual excitement, enthusiasm, a willingness to give all to the Lord. It always brings glory to Jesus. even if a prophecy corrects or calls one to forgiveness, this is a positive message from the Lord for the growth of the community or person."

Prophecy is forth-telling of the mind and heart of God to His people. Prophecy may manifest in the form of words, a vision, and thoughts or be prompted by a form of physical sensation to alert the hearer to listen. A person has this gift must fully yield to the authority and order of the event and yield to the authority for discernment. We have to endeavor to discern the message that is spoken, not necessarily accepting everything that is said as gospel truth. Prophecy should always be discerned and tested by the Community.

We must note that Prophecy is not a divine ability which someone receives to prophesy at will, but giving a definite message at a particular time by the Spirit for a distinct purpose. It is not everyone who prophesy that is a prophet (cf. 1 Cor. 14:31). A prophet, however, is a person who consistently expresses prophetic messages which are powerful and may elicit a response from the audience. Sometimes, the word may be for an individual, a group of individuals or the whole community. Prophecy can enlighten all who hear it about certain Graces to seek from God, an action to undertake, attitudes to develop or to remove from one's life or events to prepare for.

Prophecy ought not to be confused with fortune telling, which is not a gift from God. It is to help us to live our lives by the will of God and to enable us to be His witnesses in our time, bearing in mind what the Scripture says in the book of Amos 3:7. "Indeed, the Lord God does nothing without revealing it to his servants, the prophets. He always wishes to carry us along.

Dynamic or Power Gifts

Faith

The gift of Faith gives the one who receives it supernatural enablement to confidently believe without a doubt what is spoken or undertaken in Jesus' name. Faith involves entrusting oneself wholly to God and to believe absolutely and completely what He reveals.

This supernatural faith is different from 'saving or justifying faith' (Matthew 13:3-8, 18-23); which is just a basic trust in God for salvation and involves the submission of one's will to the Lordship of Jesus (Romans 5:1-2); faith in God – belief in the nature and essence of God and his everlasting love faith as fruit of the Spirit, faithfulness to God regardless of circumstances but no connection with ministry gifts (Galatians 5:22); ministry faith , given to help us use our motivational gifts (Romans 12:2-8). The gift of the Faith is the supernatural faith that will heal, bring about miracles, and move mountains! It is given spontaneously and lasts long enough for God's purpose of the moment to be accomplished. The manifestation of this kind of faith may be seen when in person knows with certainty that what he or she is praying for or hoping for will come to pass, even when the immediate happening points to a contrary reality (cf. Hebrews 11:1).

St. Peter manifested the gift of faith when he ministered to the lame man at the Beautiful Gate. In the ministry of Jesus, you find a demonstration of the power of faith. His prayer at raising Lazarus from the dead is filled with confidence. One can yield to this gift by a life of prayer and reading the Scripture. Scripture says that faith comes from hearing the Word (Romans 10:17).

Gifts of Healing (Divine Healing)

The gift of Healing is a demonstration of a supernatural outpouring of the power of God that results in the healing of diseases, infirmities, and sickness without the use of medical means. This can involve sickness of the body, soul or spirit.

God is interested in healing our total person. This healing is not restricted to the human body but the totality of human experiences, thereby fulfilling the prophecy of Isaiah (Isa. 61:1-3) which Jesus says has been fulfilled (cf. Luke 4:18-21).

Consequently, it is operational now to bring glad tidings to the poor both materially and spiritually, proclaiming liberty to captives; freeing all who are held in bondage to sin and illness by Satan, recovery of sight to the blind which encompasses physical and spiritually blindness, to let the oppressed go free from all encumbrances; whether it be inner healing or healing of memories also, to bind up those whose hearts that are broken through relationships and to proclaim the Lord's Lord acceptable year of favor; the year of Jubilee whereby, slaves are set free, debts are forgiving and properties restored.

Jesus in his ministry manifested different methods of healing, such as laying on of hands, casting out demons, spitting and making mud then applying it, and proclaiming healing from a distance. Healing usually builds up, encourage, strengthen, and make an individual or a Community new or whole for the blessing of God's people and the glory of His name. Healing increases faith serves as a sign of the presence and power of God and the growth of the Church. Healing may be physical, spiritual, psychological, emotional or relational. Sometimes, we may not receive exactly what we asked for, at such moments, we must remember that it is the will of God that will always prevail. Healing is sometimes accompanied with the gift of tears. Joy also often accompanies healing and can be expressed through "holy laughter" or tears.

This gift is made manifest when the Lord makes a person whole physical, mental or spiritual health as a direct answer to prayer. The healing can be instantaneous or gradual. We must know that the gift of Healing is not meant to substitute for natural ministries of healing exercised by the medical profession. We are, however, encouraged to seek prayers for healing. (James 5:14-15). Jesus and the Apostles used healings as tangible proof of God's presence among his people. As a precautionary measure, discernment of all the circumstances of the Gift of Healing is necessary. Those in the Healing Ministry should as a matter of necessity, receive continuous teaching, constant prayer and the being open to the other manifestation or charismatic gifts, especially Word of Knowledge and Word of Prophecy.

Gifts of Miracle (Working of Miracle)

Miracles are interventions in nature that are verifiable and which ordinarily contradicts the laws of nature. Through the exercise of the gift of working of miracles, the power of God is made manifest to produce works which go beyond the natural, overriding natural laws. Some Biblical examples include the changing of water into wine, multiplication of the loaves and fishes, healing beyond the ordinary, such as healing the withered hand (cf. Luke 6:6-10). More so; the replacement of an organ, making the blind person to see without surgery, the disappearance of a tumor without surgery. All the preceding are clear examples of the working of miracles.

Very often, the Lord bestows miracles to strengthen the faith of His people or to correct a given situation which cannot be accomplished by any natural means; or to show His power at work in response to a ministry of preaching or teaching. A miracle brings about awe and wonders at God's power so that glory is given to God. Miracles, which always happen instantaneously, are a much more powerful sign of God's presence and action than healings, which may be instantaneous, gradual or a quick recovery. The gift of Faith certainly has to be manifest in the working of miracles when one gives a command in Jesus name without any doubt.

This gift would include that of raising the dead(Acts 9:36-41) Such displays of God's power in the apostolic era caused much fear among those that witnessed them and thus promoted the activity of the Holy Spirit to bring many people into the Church in those days and even in our time. Some examples may include; healing of a terminal disease, Miracles of Philip in Samaria (cf. Acts 8:6), the raising of Eutychus from the dead (cf. Acts 20:10), Paul's safety after being bitten by the snake (cf. Acts 28:5)

It is a truth that not all members of the body have the same function. The ministry gifts are the gifts of function or position in the body of Christ. In St. Paul's' letter to the Ephesians (Eph. 4:11-12), he affirmed these ministry gifts when he says that the Holy Spirit "gave some to be apostles, others as prophets, others as evangelists, others as pastors and teachers, to enlighten the holy ones for the work of ministry, for building up the body of Christ."(Eph. 4:11-12). The five ministry gifts are the leaders God gives to teach and inspire us in our Christian mission. St. Paul says that God has given these ministry gifts to the church to enrich the people of God for their work of building up the Body of Christ. These gifts include the following:

Apostle

This is one of the hierarchical gifts (Greek Word: Apostolos -'apo'-from 'Stello'-send; one sent forth). One who is sent forth to new frontiers with the gospel divinely enabled to provide leadership over Church Communities and exercise authority over spiritual matters that pertain to the Body of Christ. It is a ministry gift that enables the one who receives it exercise the gift and function in the office of an Apostle.

Prophet

This is one who perceives the will of God. The prophet's corresponding gift is prophecy, which is reporting something that God spontaneously brings to the mind of the prophet. This may also take the form of foretelling the future as in Acts 11:27-28.

Evangelizer (Evangelist)

This gift enables the one who receives it to function in the office of an Evangelizer; An Evangelizer goes from place to place spreading the good news of the Gospel message. His or her ultimate business is the salvation of the others. St. Paul is a good example of those who fulfill this ministry.

Pastor

The office or role of a Pastor is that of overseeing the Spiritual welfare of the Body of Christ This gift falls under the category/group of Administrative Gifts, it fortifies its bearer with grace to be responsible for spiritually caring, for protecting, guiding, and feeding a group of believers entrusted to his or her care. The overseer also will have a spiritual sense and ability to know the problems of the Community, the direction the Spirit of God is leading, and he will know what to do to preserve the believers in a proper spiritual condition in every difficulty.

Teaching

Rom 12:7; 1 Cor. 12:28; Eph.4:11 The gift of teaching gives one the disposition to instruct others in the Bible in a logical, systematic way to communicate pertinent information for true understanding and growth. Teaching gift gives the one who receives it an ability to take the Word of God and open its truths spiritually for the edification of the believers. Teaching is distinct from prophecy for the fact that the teacher does not receive what he or she teaches and the material as a direct revelation from God, but he or she has to study the Word of God and wait on the Lord to get a message and the knowledge to teach the Community.

The teaching gift does not end with personal comprehension; it is beyond that. It is an ability to communicate your comprehension properly and effectively to others who listen. It is the ability to impart spiritual truth and give the proper sense to the Word of God. Some may be good students but may not be able to express what they have been taught such that those who listen to them can grasp what they teach and are edified. The teacher can take the hard and difficult things of the Word of God and break them down into easily understandable bits that are suitable for all irrespective of their level of understanding.

The Reason behind the Gifts of the Holy Spirit

So that she can fulfill her mission, the Holy Spirit 'bestows upon the Church varied hierarchic and charismatic gifts, and this way directs her.' However, the Church, endowed with the gifts of her founder and faithfully observing his precepts of charity, humility, and self-denial, receives the mission of proclaiming and establishing among all peoples the Kingdom of Christ and God, and she is on earth the seed and the beginning of that kingdom"(CCC. 768).

The Holy Spirit 'distributes special graces among the faithful of every rank' for the building up of the Church. When these gifts are used with careful discernment of spirits and obedience, they are "fitting and useful for the needs of the Church."

Management of the Gifts

St. Paul notes that there are different kinds of gifts but the same Spirit. There are different kinds of service, but the same Lord (1 Cor. 12:4-5). Everyone is to use whatever gift he or she has to serve others, faithfully administering God's grace in its various forms (1 Peter). In just the same way as each of us has one body with many members, and these different parts do not all have the same function. Likewise, in Christ, we who are many forms one body, and each member belongs to all the others. We are to exercise our gifts, according to the grace given to us. (Rom. 12:4-6).

Disparity in Number of Gifts

Although there are different opinions on the actual number of spiritual gifts, God's Word indicates a variety of gifts. This implies that the emphasis is not on how many they are but to establish the fact that the Spirit gives gifts as He wishes and in the number, He wishes, usually subject to the need of a particular Community or Church.

How to Use the Gifts

The essence of the gifts are for the common good of the Church and must not be used for self gratification promote the importance of the person bearing the gift. We are the vehicles the Lord uses to release His blessings upon His people. We are the 'gift bearers' and must function "with humility, willingness to take risks, trust in God, and love for our brothers and sisters in Christ." All who have these gifts have to bear in mind that the gift is not for keeps but service. The intention of the Giver must always be respected.

The Holy Spirit's gifts are freely given to us so we will fulfill the God-given purpose of our lives. The Church in her teaching holds that "Charisms are to be accepted with gratitude by the person who receives them and all members of the Church too. They are a wonderfully rich grace for the apostolic nourishment and the holiness of the Body of Christ, so long as they are genuine gifts of the Holy Spirit and are used in conformity with authentic promptings of this same Spirit, that is, in keeping with charity, the true measure of all charisms." More so, "discernment of charisms is necessary, always. No gift is exempt from being referred to and submitted to the Church's shepherds. Their office is not indeed to extinguish the Spirit but put to all things to the test, and retain only what is right so that all the diverse and complementary gifts work together 'for the common good (CCC. 800-801).

Distribution of Charismatic Gifts

We have already stated that the Holy Spirit gives spiritual gifts to people. However, the Charismatic Gift is not given to an individual believer on merits. It is not because one is more significant than another child of God that he or she receives a specific gift. The gifts are given according to the infinite knowledge, wisdom, and purpose of God (I Cor.12:11). The Spirit of God by Himself gives every believer; individually, or in particular according to His will alone. This means it is outside the realm of man's choice or determination altogether to choose gifts.

The Holy Spirit gives Charismatic gifts to be used for the blessing of others and to further God's purpose to complete the church. Those gifts are exercised in evangelization as God works to reach the lost. They are put to use in the assembly and other believers to build up Christians by teaching and personal ministry to them. Through these gifts given to men, God's blessing can be manifested and realized. A gift is not exercised privately or toward the individual who has the gift in the sense of using a gift for personal enjoyment. The gift is intended to be exercised in ministry toward others. Some, out of selfishness, greed, and ignorance, tend to exercise the gift privately for their own enjoyment or blessing. This view has no ground in God's Word. No Charismatic gift is intended to be used privately or for personal benefit.

Charismatic Gifts are to be used under the direction of the Holy Spirit are subject to God intends it to be used for. That gift is a "manifestation of the Spirit" (I Cor. 12:7), and

He purposes to accomplish some essential work through that gift for the blessing of His Children, the building up of the body of Christ, through strengthening of the local assembly and the evangelization of the lost (Eph. 4:12-15; I Cor. 14:24-26).

Where to Use the Gifts

Charismatic gifts are to be used to build up the body of Christ from within the Community. That is, they are internally oriented. The gift of evangelization is an extension of the gospel activity of an assembly. The gift will be exercised to further the Community by the salvation of precious souls and their being brought into its fellowship or by anticipating the work God will do in saving souls so that a Community might be established.

Those who have received the gifts of the Holy Spirit should always bear in mind the purpose for which the Holy Spirit has raised them up and given them. It is not for selfish position and love of prominence or popularity, but rather to completely hand over to God. Having a gift with its heavy responsibility should make us fully disposed to increasingly develop and exercise it entirely and adequately in the time we are allowed for our ministry. The essence of the gifts of the Holy Spirit as intended by its giver is the maturing of believers, the building up of that body of Christ to completion so that through the ministry of these gifts, it grows to maturity.

Gift Management Guide

As an addendum, you ought to adhere to the following gift management guide:

Practice daily prayer and quiet time with the Lord.

Meet regularly with believers to pray together. For Catholics, this can be done through regular Mass attendance as well as being a committed member of a prayer group of the Catholic Charismatic Renewal. More so, ensure you belong to a Ministry.

Spend quality time each day studying the Scriptures.

You must be determined to accept Jesus as your personal Lord and Master as well as being faithful to his teachings

CHAPTER SIX

CONCLUSION

The Holy Spirit is given so that believers who receive Him may exercise the power of God ultimately as Jesus did while on earth. Little wonder, Jesus says to his disciples; "Do not leave Jerusalem, but wait for the gift I told you about, the gift my Father promised" (Acts 1:4). More so, He emphasizes; but when the Holy Spirit shall come upon you, you will receive power and will be witnesses for me in Jerusalem, in all Judea and Samaria, even to the earth's end (cf. Acts 1:8).

It is therefore apparent that the whole Christian experiences; from new birth to resurrection, both individually and corporately is bound up in the working of the Holy Spirit. When we overlook His vital role in our lives, it is to our spiritual detriment. The Holy Spirit gives believers every enabling grace to appropriate the promises of God and to put His power to use.

Pope Francis insists that we need to let ourselves be imbued with the light of the Holy Spirit so that He introduces us into the Truth of God, who is the only Lord of our lives.

BIBLIOGRAPHY

The Catechism of the Catholic Church (2002) Revised edition India.PaulinesPublicaiton.

Made in the USA
Monee, IL
08 April 2022

94382996R10094